PRAISE FOR TOUCHPOiNT POWER

From Noted Authors and Thought-Leaders

The deliberate process of architecting experiences to deliver at critical customer touchpoints is fundamental to the craft and discipline of customer experience. Hank's book will be a great resource to support embedding that skill inside your organization.

Jeanne Bliss
Author, Chief Customer Officer and President, CustomerBliss
Co-founder, Customer Experience Professionals Association

As one of the pioneers of Customer Experience industry and having written four books on Customer Experience, I have seen many companies get journey mapping very wrong. *TOUCHPOiNT POWER* gets it right. It shows how mapping touchpoints should be used for building a consistently great Customer Experience.

Colin Shaw
Founder & CEO, Beyond Philosophy

Every touchpoint as an opportunity to build a stronger relationship with a brand. *TOUCHPOiNT POWER* helps companies understand exactly how to identify, improve and measure key touchpoints to consistently deliver positive customer/ brand experiences. This promotes deeper brand knowledge and advocacy, driving growth and revenue.

David Wisnom III
Founder & CEO SightCast Inc.
Co-author Before the Brand: Creating the Unique
DNA of an Enduring Brand Identity

TOUCHPOiNT POWER will help you build customer centricity. Everyone that is committed to driving a service culture will learn a lot from the book. Today many firms believe they are awesome at service. As Hank said, "Your customers must be able to tell or perceive a difference." To achieve this important differentiation, master the principles in *TOUCHPOiNT POWER*.

John Tschohl
President & Founder, Service Quality Institute
Author of Excellence Through Customer Service

From Business Leaders

TOUCHPOiNT POWER is an outstanding guide that will help you translate customer-centric ideas into a serious, sustainable differentiator. Hank Brigman delivers a disciplined methodology that is as practical as it is visionary. Whether you occupy the back office, the front line, or the C-suite, the *TOUCHPOiNT POWER* approach offers excellent tools to apply at every level of your organization.

Scott Shober
Principal, Ducker Worldwide

TOUCHPOiNT POWER is a practical guide to help any organization of any size develop and implement a customer-focused strategy. I know first-hand the wealth of experience Hank brings to guide this process, avoid common pitfalls, and maximize success. Chock full of ideas and tips, Hank's book will help take your organization to new heights and win and retain more customers.

Paul Hemburrow
President, Paro Marketing Strategy

The success of any company lies in its ability to maximize client relations. Through straightforward, practical steps, *TOUCHPOiNT POWER* delivers the goods. Get a jump on your competition by reading this book. Your clients will thank you again and again.

John Ryan
Vice President, Ketchum Public Relations

For over six years we have used Hank's methodologies to improve patient retention and referrals, and our practice's profitability. Through RealPatientRatings™, we are now helping other practices gather voice of patient data so that they too can improve retention, referrals and profitability, touchpoint by touchpoint.

Marie B.V. Olesen
CEO, La Jolla Cosmetic Surgery Centre
Founder, Chief Patient Experience Officer, The Real Ratings Group, LLC.

The increased ability to connect is driving today's customer revolution. *TOUCHPOiNT POWER* is your guide to successfully managing these connections and becoming a "customer company."

Alex Bard
SVP and GM, Service Cloud, salesforce.com

A brilliant book by a customer experience pioneer. This hands-on guide is a must read for those who want to win the hearts and minds of their customers.

Joep Wijman
President of WijmanCoaching, Netherlands

TOUCHPOiNT POWER teaches Hank Brigman's proven method for delivering a consistent and measurable customer experience. It is like drinking from a fire hose of customer experience knowledge – I made pages of notes. This book provides you with the knowledge and tools to build a competitive advantage and get and keep more patients/customers.

Walt West
OD, Fellow of the American Academy of Optometry

New devices and new applications create a world where your customer holds the power of touchpoints in their hands, 24x7. *TOUCHPOINT POWER* teaches you how to create value for both customer and organization at this and other key touchpoints – deepening your customer's relationship with your organization.

Matthew Trifiro
CMO Heroku, salesforce.com

From Customer Experience Professionals

Customer-centricity has rapidly become the most important way to achieve a differentiated competitive advantage. We have found that Brigman's practical approach to customer-centricity engages and empowers people throughout our organization. Apply *TOUCHPOiNT POWER* to differentiate, and to enhance both customer and employee satisfaction and loyalty.

Lars A. Janson
Vice President Global Customer Experience

TOUCHPOiNT POWER provides the methodologies, resources and tools to accelerate your customer engagement practice. A must have for any customer experience professional.

Diane Magers
Customer Experience Executive

The practical application of customer experience concepts is going to make this book a go-to reference for any organization.

Sandra Fornasier
Director, Customer Experience, Ciena Corporation, Canada

TOUCHPOiNT POWER is a must-read structural approach to developing and implementing a Customer Experience Strategy across all touchpoints. You will learn exactly how to consistently deliver customer experiences that match your brand and values, and that wow your customers.

Remy Simonis
Owner, Customer Management Adviesgroep, Netherlands

From Sales Professionals

A focused and structured approach is needed to get and keep the customer at the center of any organization's efforts. It is great to finally have a book that provides a systematic approach to building that structure, supporting field sales, and achieving the true value of customer-centricity.

Jackie Beckenbach
Regional Director Corporate and Independent Accounts, Glaxo Smith Kline

I've had the privilege of working with Hank to develop our strategy to improve our customer experience and his results were nothing short of remarkable. His Touchpoint approach is exactly what we needed and it worked! I highly recommend this book and more importantly, utilizing his tools to improve your customer experience.

Jack Rawle
Senior Director, Worldwide Sales Operations & Effectiveness

TOUCHPOINT
POWER!

TOUCHPOINT POWER!

**Get & Keep More Customers
Touchpoint by Touchpoint**

Hank Brigman

Foreword by Peppers & Rogers

William Henry
publishing

William Henry Publishing • Atlantic Beach, FL

TOUCHPOiNT POWER!

Published by, William Henry Publishing
P.O. Box 330800
Atlantic Beach, FL 32233, USA

Publisher's Cataloging-in-Publication data

Brigman, Hank.
   Touchpoint power : how to get and keep more customers touchpoint by touchpoint / Hank Brigman.
   p. cm.
   ISBN 978-0-9673652-3-7
   Includes bibliographical references and index.

1. Customer service. 2. Customer relations. 3. Success in business. I. Title.

HF5415.5 .B745 2013
658.8/12 --dc23   2013934234

Book Design by Pamela Terry, Opus 1 Design

Printed in United States of America

ACKNOWLEDGEMENTS

I found that it takes more than a village to successfully complete a book. For their feedback or support or inspiration, I would like to thank Carol Alexander, Jennifer Battalin, Bill Brigman, Janie Brigman, Chris Curtis, Stephanie Curtis, Janice Dody, Steve Dykstra, Lynne Elliott, Lyman Fletcher, Robert Fortunato, Scott Friedman, John Geolz, Jana Johns, Mark Kraus, Pat Larky, Dennis Magruder, Don Mellott, Jr., Rick Merritt, Mary Morris, Marie Olesen, Mike Osorio, Tom Pavlik, Bruce Perkins, Gretchen Perkins, Jim Poirot, Boone Powell, Jack Querio, Deb Scaringi, Crystal Sheeler, Jim Stoddard, Matt Trifiro, Dick Wallingford, and David Wood.

Special thanks for their feedback to Jackie Beckenbach, Richard Clompus, Maureen Cook, Suzanne Donnels, Stefan Ferrara, Sandra Fornasier, Glenn Gunter, Patrick Hanson, Paul Hemburrow, Vicki Hess, Lars Janson, Firas Jarrar, John King, Kristofer Lindbak, Jan Petter Lindbak, Victoria Lindbak, Diane Magers, Joe Matton, George McCann, Brenna Milonas, Jason Parry, John Ryan, Scott Shober, Martin Skeer, Tana Still, Walt West, and David Wisnom.

As for feedback, there have been several along for the entire ride. They actually read multiple versions of the manuscript – imagine that. Huge thanks to Jon Obermeyer, Matt Soergel, and Jack Rawle. Gargantuan thanks to Jan Larkey. I estimate she read at least eight versions, providing outstanding feedback and support with each read.

On the production and promotion side of things, thanks to Sukhjit Ghag, Victoria Harrell, Mary Harper, Pam Terry, Mary Ann Stein Raulerson, Jeff Schneider and Matt Trifiro.

I have been encouraged by so many who helped light the torch for Customer Experience Management and/or continue to ensure that it burns bright. This includes, but I am sure is not limited to, Ken Blanchard, Jeanne Bliss, Lou Carbone, Jim Collins, W. Edwards Deming,

Peter Drucker, Donna Fluss, Jeffrey Gitomer, Shep Hyken, Joseph Michelli, Don Peppers, Tom Peters, B. Joseph Pine, Fred Reichheld, Martha Rogers, Bruce Temkin, Colin Shaw and Shaun Smith.

Lastly, this book would not have been possible without the support of my wife, Kathryn. Beautiful inside and out, she is the strongest person I know. Her strength and inner beauty inspire me both personally and and professionally.

To my wife, Kathryn

SUMMARY TABLE OF CONTENTS

Hank Brigman

Detailed Table of Contents

Section I — 23
Customer Experience (CX)
The Core Customer Experience Problem and its Solution

Chapter 1: The Problem. 27
The Core Customer Experience Problem and How Organizations Perpetuate this Problem

Chapter 2: The Solution. 39
Customer Experience Management (CEM) and its Foundations

Section II — 61
The Three Competencies of
Customer-Centric Organizations
A Deep Dive into the Competencies your Organization Must Build in Order to Become Customer-Centric

Chapter 3: The Identity Competency.
Define and Live Your Identity

---

[1] Net Promoter® and NPS® are registered trademarks of Bain & Company, Inc., Fred Reichheld and Satmetrix Systems, Inc.

Section III — 103
How To Achieve Customer-Centricity
A Proven Implementation Model for
Getting & Keeping More Customers

Chapter 6: A Proven Implementation Model. 109
A Company at a Crossroad and Their Choice of How To
Differentiate & Build a Defendable Competitive Advantage

Chapter 7: Model Step 1, Assess. 119
Auditing the Current State

Section IV — 229
Resources

*Touchpoint Naming Convention, Valuable Formula
and Availability of Additional Resources*

xvii

Touchpoint:
Each interaction –
physical, communication,
human and sensory – with
and within your organization.

*To your customers, you **are** your touchpoints*

Author's Statement

My professional Vision is to serve the global need to improve the lives of customers, employees and employers. Customer Experience Management (CEM) is the new discipline by which all organizations can achieve customer-centricity – and advance this Vision.

Through TOUCHPOiNT POWER, I share my knowledge, methodologies and tools to assist you in building a customer-centric team, department or business. In doing so, I hope that together we further the young discipline of CEM and improve the lives of customers, employees and employers.

In support of my professional Vision, I will donate at least 10% of the net proceeds from TOUCHPOiNT POWER to a not-for-profit association that shares this Vision. Visit *www.TouchpointPower.com/Vision* to learn about the supported organization.

At Your Service,

xxi

OVERVIEW

Business Purpose: *"The purpose of business is to get and keep customers."* Peter Drucker, management guru

Problem Statement: Inconsistent and/or negative touchpoints inhibit the ability to get and keep desired customers and employees, negatively impacting financial metrics.

Value Proposition: As a result of applying the information, methodologies and tools in *TOUCHPOiNT POWER*, you will learn exactly how to build three competencies and the structure needed to successfully ask four questions for *each touchpoint*:

1. ***Customer.*** What is the customer trying to accomplish – what do they need, want or value at this touchpoint?

2. ***Identity.*** How can we best meet customer needs and wants – make it easier for them – while advancing (or not detracting from) our Values, Identity and Experience Strategy? How do we want our customer to feel?

3. ***Touchpoint.*** What are our goals with this touchpoint and how can we accomplish them?

4. ***Best practice.*** What current and/or potential best practice would "wow" the customer?

Implementing, promoting and measuring the results will solve the problem and advance achieving the business purpose, improving financial performance.

Applicability: No matter your organization's size or geographical reach – or what you call your customers (clients, donors, patients, students, constituents, etc.) – or whether your goal is just to improve customer satisfaction, address specific customer experiences, or to build a customer-centric culture – the principles, methodologies and tools presented in *TOUCHPOiNT POWER* are applicable for:

- Individuals
- Groups, departments, divisions, operating companies
- Entire organizations

FOREWORD

By Don Peppers and Martha Rogers, Ph.D.

As you begin to read *TOUCHPOiNT POWER*, and to think about the future of your business, you will be deeply aware of the inexorable march of technology.

The extremely rapid improvements in computer technology that have delivered your business to this point are driven by "Moore's Law," which suggests that every 15 to 20 years computers get a thousand times more powerful, as the computer industry figures out how to squeeze more and more transistors onto the same tiny slivers of silicon.

But there is a corollary to Moore's Law sometimes known as "Zuckerberg's Law," which suggests that every 15 to 20 years we interact a thousand times as much with others. We will report our good and bad experiences across an expanding array of social platforms, and many of the stories we tell will be about companies we do business with. As interactions increase in both volume and speed, we will demand more and more trustworthiness from those we interact with. After all, trust allows us to interact more efficiently. We don't have to check sources or verify details, and we can rely on what we learn immediately, whether we're ordering a product, deciding to see a movie, paying a bill, or taking a trip. Untrustworthy interactions, by contrast, are just a hassle. They waste our time.

We will want to do more business with – and recommend to others – the companies we trust. But before we trust a business we have to respect both the company's intentions and its competence. Is it only watching out for itself, or is it watching out for us, too? And does it have the competence to carry out these good intentions? Moreover, as we document in our new book *Extreme Trust: Honesty as a Competitive Advantage* (Penguin, 2012), the increased speed and volume of interactions mean that today's customers are already demanding an even higher standard of trustworthiness from the companies they buy from. They demand *proactive* trustworthiness, or what we call "trustability." If a customer is about to make a mistake and pay more than he needs to, or if he's about to overlook a late fee deadline, for instance, he expects a company to remind him or warn him – i.e., to watch out for his interests, and not just for the company's own profit.

Zuckerberg's Law implies that in 15 to 20 years you will have a *thousand times* as many touchpoints with each of your individual customers as you have today. So if you want your business to thrive in a future driven by thousands of times as much customer interaction, a future in which customers expect *Extreme Trust*, then your first step should be to understand how your business touches the customer today, and how you can harness the power that these touchpoints represent for your business.

In our MBA-level textbook on CRM, *Managing Customer Relationships: A Strategic Perspective* (Wiley, 2nd edition, 2011), we rely on a kind of four-step process for helping students to understand what it takes to set up and manage customer relationships. We call this four-step method the "IDIC" process – for *identifying* customers, *differentiating* them, *interacting* with them, and *customizing* for them – and it neatly summarizes the mechanics of the customer relationship management task.

The first two steps – identifying and differentiating customers – have to do with customer data. It's of course impossible to have a "relationship" with a market segment or a population. You can only enjoy a relationship with an individual, which means the very first step is identifying your individual customers. If you don't know the identities of individual customers when they come into your store or when they buy a product through your distributor, then you can't very well initiate a relationship, right? You don't necessarily need to know every customer's name or phone number, but if you want to manage a relationship then you have to know it's the same customer in the store today who was interacting with you last night on the Web or at the call center.

Moreover, each of these customers is unique and different, with needs and preferences that are all their own. And they represent different values to you, too, in terms of their likely future business. So in addition to individual identifying data, you must also be able to *differentiate* your customers in terms of their needs and their values. What a customer wants, and what he's worth to you – that's both sides of the customer value proposition. All other descriptions of customer differences – demographics, psychographics, transactional histories – are just attempts to get at these two basic differences.

So the first two steps, identify and differentiate, are the "thinking" part of managing a customer relationship. Done behind the scenes, these two steps culminate in "customer insight." Developing this customer insight is sometimes called "analytical CRM," but an important point is that the customer doesn't participate in it, and may not even be aware that your business is collecting and analyzing transactional and other data in order to better understand who each individual customer is and how he or she is different from or similar to other customers.

But the second two steps – interacting with and customizing for customers – directly involve the customer. A company can't interact with a customer without the customer's actual awareness and participation in the interaction. Interactions of all kinds are "touchpoints" that have a direct bearing on the relationship between customer and company. And when the company customizes its treatment of a customer based on the insight it already has as well as any interactions with the customer, that treatment is yet another vital touchpoint. These touchpoints accumulate in the customer's mind, and the sum total of them could be thought of as the "customer experience."

If identifying and differentiating customers are the components of "analytical CRM," then interacting with customers and customizing for them represent "operational CRM." And operational CRM, or customer experience management, requires tracking and managing a company's individual "touchpoints" with individual customers. With *TOUCHPOiNT POWER*, our colleague Hank Brigman has written a book designed to help you manage your customer touchpoints so as to provide each of your customers with the best possible kind of overall experience.

The "IDIC" Method
for Managing Customer Relationships

Identify
...customers as uniquely
addressable individuals

Differentiate
...by individual
needs and value

Customer *Insight*

Interact
...cost-efficiently
and effectively

Customize
...the company's
offerings or behavior

Customer *Experience*

TOUCHPOiNT POWER

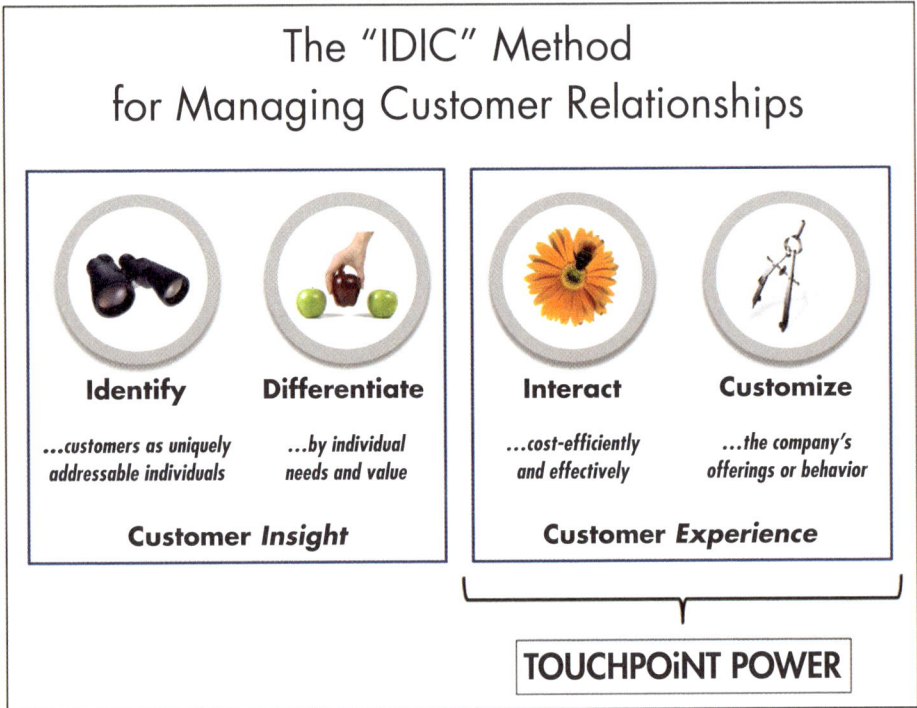

To get the most "TOUCHPOiNT POWER" you will have to change the behaviors of your own executives, managers, and employees. You have to ensure that the leaders at your firm are enthusiastically on board with you. We once brainstormed this issue with a Fortune 500 CEO who was wrestling with the issue, and together we outlined six different "behaviors" that would characterize the executives at such a firm. To maximize your own company's "TOUCHPOiNT POWER," your executives should:

1. *Accumulate expertise* in the area of customer-focused strategies and relationship management, and become an informal "cheerleader" for the ideas involved. Managing your customers' experiences more effectively will require not just computer technology but also new marketing, sales and customer service tactics. Very few companies are yet doing business this way, so the disciplines required are not very well known. A leader will make it his or her business to find out more about being customer-centric, attending workshops or seminars, reading books and articles, and calling in experts – becoming fluent in the new thinking around TOUCHPOiNT POWER and facilitating that fluency so everyone has a common language and philosophy.

2. *Sponsor pilot projects* and shelter the people involved in them. Your company's transformation must be engineered and implemented in pieces, if it is to be successful at all. Pilot projects designed to prove the concept and measure benefits will be required, but in budget-tight times a loss-producing pilot can easily get jettisoned. A leader who believes in building valuable customer relationships and supports this transformation to TOUCHPOiNT POWER will provide sponsorship for proof-of-concept pilot projects even when they lose money.

3. *Measure success differently*, establishing not just new metrics, but also new reward structures. A leader will root out inconsistencies and conflicts in the company's rewards and incentives programs, and try to create a better alignment with the goal of improving every customer's experience with the brand.

4. *Cross boundaries* in order to try to generate enterprise-wide results. Customer-specific actions are often not product-specific or business-unit-specific. When the enterprise seeks to treat different customers differently, in an integrated way across all touchpoints, there will be conflicts among departments and functions. Leaders recognize this and will actively cross boundaries in order to make the new processes work.

5. *Make direct contact with customers.* In the final analysis, customers are the "power" in TOUCHPOiNT POWER. Customers are at the very center of the transformation you are seeking. Your leaders will recognize this, and they will want to meet customers, talk with them, watch the focus groups, visit the customer sites, and so forth. There is no substitute for direct experience.

6. *Communicate and live by customer-oriented values.* The CEO and senior management team have an overriding and indispensable role in both communicating the values of the company to employees and others, and in reinforcing them with their everyday behavior. Formal communication is the easy part – you do that with policies, tools, training, and performance measurements. But values are also communicated in the actions and behaviors of senior managers themselves. (We met a CEO who told his executives he wanted them to build customer value, but

every morning his first question was "How much product did you move yesterday?") If you want to harvest the value of each customer's relationship, then your employees must know, both formally and informally, that above all else your company values taking the customer's perspective, in order to earn and keep the customer's trust.

The only revenue your company will ever generate will come from customers, by definition. No product, or brand, or store, or patent pays money. Only customers do – the ones you have now, and the ones you will have in the future. The amount they choose to spend with you will be the defining limit on the size of your business. What TOUCHPOiNT POWER is all about is helping to build the greatest value for each of these customers of yours, in order to realize the full value potential for your company.

PREFACE

Insights into the Dynamic Macro Changes
In the Marketplace and How Closing the
Strategy-to-Touchpoint Gap Will Help
You Succeed in Our New World

PREFACE

As a result of reading the Preface you will better understand the power of touchpoints and why there are so few customer-centric organizations. You will gain insights into the macro dynamics at play in the marketplace that impact which of the three differentiation options is best for your organization:

- Quality/innovation
- Price
- Service/experience

You will understand how *TOUCHPOiNT POWER* is laid out, my credibility in this space and how *TOUCHPOiNT POWER* will benefit you and your efforts.

Preface/The Power of Touchpoints
Some people "get" customer-centricity

Gavin Merritt is in his usual First Class seat. A regular on this flight, he smiles as Captain Denny Flanagan acknowledges him with his familiar hello. As Captain Flanagan passes, Gavin can't help but appreciate the hand-written notes Captain Flanagan has passed to him thanking him for being a United frequent flyer. Despite the fact that other carriers are occasionally

less expensive on this route, Gavin chooses this United flight due to the probability that Captain Flanagan will be its pilot.

An attractive woman with beautiful grey hair and a worried look on her face is in seat 9C. Her "baby," Mac, a 9-year-old frisky Scot Terrier, is in the plane's hold. Captain Flanagan walks up and asks, "Ms. Jenkins, what is the name of your lovely Scot Terrier?" "Mac," she replies, startled. Captain Flanagan reaches for his mobile phone. "Take a look at this picture. As you can see, Mac is doing great down in our pet lounge. I want you to know that we are going to get you both to Chicago safe and sound." The relief on Ms. Jenkins face is quickly replaced by a beaming smile and a heartfelt, "Thank you."

A single father gets a call

Ian Janson is wringing his hands in Chicago. He hates to fly. On this day, it isn't his flight he is worried about. He's a single father, and his daughter, Maria, is returning from a two-week stay with his parents. Ian is pouring another cup of coffee when the phone rings. "Mr. Janson?" "Yes" he answers quizzically. "This is Captain Denny Flanagan. I am the pilot of Maria's flight today to Chicago. I just spoke to her and she is doing great. I just want you to know that we are going to take great care of your daughter for you. The weather looks good and I should have her to you on time. You can trust that she is in caring hands." Ian voices his appreciation, sits down, sighs, and slowly raises the steaming cup of coffee to his lips. Ahhh.[2]

Today, more than ever, it is important to be customer-centric. Captain Denny Flanagan is customer-centric — he gets it. These touchpoints are powerful in their ability to generate positive results from customers. But today it is not about a single employee delivering great service. Today, as organizations seek to differentiate and gain competitive advantages, it is about *how* to build customer-centricity into the very fabric of the organization's DNA. It's *not* about *how* to build an organization of Denny Flanagans. It's about *how* to build the competencies and structure such that all employees consistently develop and deliver touchpoints like Denny Flanagan.

> It's not about how to build an organization of Denny Flanagans. It's about how to build the competencies and structure such that all employees consistently develop and deliver touchpoints like Denny Flanagan.

---

[2] These narratives are examples based on documented practices of United Airline Captain Denny Flanagan

Hank Brigman

Preface/Differentiation

Eeny, meeny, miny moe, which differentiator to choose?

There is a need to differentiate, but which differentiation option is best? The ability to differentiate has historically filtered down to bucket into one of three options:

- Quality/innovation
- Price
- Service/experience

Quality/Innovation fighting "good enough"

Quality, including innovation, covers many areas including product and process. This potential differentiator is challenged by a "good enough" philosophy made even more relevant during times of economic pressures. The "good enough" situation is especially prevalent in mature markets. Is your computer fast enough such that the next improvement in speed is enough of a differentiator to get you to buy? Is your word processing or spreadsheet software good enough such that the next version with a few new enhancements is enough of a differentiator to get you to upgrade?

In maturing markets where innovation stagnates and organizations struggle to differentiate, we hear the hushed echoes of the cop-out – "commoditization."

Your customers must be able to tell or perceive a difference

A key to differentiation is to do so in a manner that your customers can either quantify or perceive a difference. The best-case is that customers can actually tell that your product or service is different or better.

I have found that highly educated professional service providers such as doctors and lawyers often have a tough time differentiating. They spent a great deal of time and effort gaining needed education and getting good at what they do. It is natural that they want to position their practice as the best – they seek to differentiate through quality.

The truth is that I can't really tell if my lawyer, doctor, accountant or even my auto mechanic is any better than the next one – I don't have the expertise in their specialty to make that determination. What I can tell is if they return my calls in a timely manner, keep their office or shop

5

clean, or bill me correctly. I do have the expertise to know when I am getting good or bad service.

Truth: While quality can be a strong differentiator, it must be both quantifiable by customers and sustainable in order to establish the coveted long-term competitive advantage.

Price is a dangerous place to differentiate

Unless you have the size and supply-chain power of a Wal-Mart, you probably don't want to differentiate through price.

Preface/Touchpoint Economy™
Introducing the Touchpoint Economy

This leaves customer service/experience. And more and more organizations are starting to look to differentiate through customer experience (CX).

As the title of this book implies, individual touchpoints are powerful in their ability to impact customer decisions, perceptions and an organization's finances. With economic pressures and the exploding use of social media to spread the word – positive and negative – regarding products and companies, it is a brand new world out there.

In this new economy – this Touchpoint Economy – businesses are facing a growing need to improve customer touchpoints and experiences in order to compete. Many savvy organizations are turning to improving customer experiences as their means of differentiating.

Touchpoint Economy
The macro environment whereby the economy of individual organizations, brands or products is highly impacted by the increasing power of customer touchpoints.

Maybe you have never heard the word touchpoint – maybe you hear it all too often. In 2007 I was the first to define "touchpoint" on the online encyclopedia, Wikipedia. Since then, my definition has gone through a natural evolution to land on the following:

> **Touchpoint:** Each interaction - physical, communication, human and sensory - with and within your organization.

If your organization makes a product, that product is an example of a physical touchpoint, something you can feel. Your ads, emails and brochures are all examples of communication touchpoints. Your sales,

service and accounting employees are examples of human touchpoints. The music you play or the aromas you create are your sensory touchpoints – think of the smell of popcorn in a movie theater.

Three outcomes of a touchpoint

As a result of a touchpoint or touchpoints, one of three things can happen. Your customer can:

- Say something good
- Say something bad
- Say nothing at all

Logic dictates that the more good touchpoints you deliver the greater the chance your customer will feel and say good things about your organization and its products or services.

The customer-centric club is small

It is hard, extremely hard, to consistently deliver great touchpoints. Think about it: Which companies in the Fortune 500 are truly customer-centric? When I ask that question of audiences, I get the usual cast of characters: Disney, Southwest Airlines, Nordstrom, L.L. Bean, The Ritz-Carlton, Virgin Atlantic, Harrah's Casino, etc. The fact is that I rarely get more than ten companies named. For the sake of argument, let's say there are twenty companies in the Fortune 500 that are truly customer-centric. That leaves 480 companies that *aren't* customer-centric. Yet each of these 480 companies *knows* that being customer-centric and providing good customer experiences, touchpoints and service is good for business, and good for their bottom line.

So why aren't there more customer-centric companies in the Fortune 500?

The philosophy that worked for baseball manager Casey Stengel, probably isn't the best way to approach your touchpoints and customers today: *"The key to being a good manager is keeping the people who hate me away from those who are still undecided."*

We need a better plan. This is especially true in today's world where a bad experience can reach millions via the internet.

The missing strategy and structure

More than a better plan, we actually need a new strategy and a new structure. Organizations have developed strategies and structures

7

around those activities and processes that are important to their success and viability. There are long-term strategies, sales strategies, marketing strategies, and even exit strategies.

There are structures for hiring employees, making and selling products, accepting payment and accounting – just to name a few.

What's missing for most organizations is an "Experience Strategy" – a strategy for how customers experience the product/service/brand. Also missing is a "Touchpoint Structure" – a structure for *how* to define and consistently deliver customer-centric touchpoints.

Experience Strategy

Why we undertake Customer Experience Management (CEM) and *what* we seek to achieve through *where* we position both our service policies and the execution of customer touchpoints and *how* customers experience our Identity.

Organizations need a structure to get to and answer four questions for each and every touchpoint, and then implement and measure the results. The four questions for each touchpoint are:

1. **Customer.** What is the customer trying to accomplish – what do they need, want or value at this touchpoint?

2. **Identity.** How can we best meet customer needs and wants – make it easier for them – while advancing (or not detracting from) our Values, Identity and Experience Strategy? How do we want our customer to feel?

3. **Touchpoint.** What are our goals with this touchpoint and how can we accomplish them?

4. **Best practice.** What current and/or potential best practice would "wow" the customer?

The iconic customer service companies have a Touchpoint Structure based on these questions. This structure is their secret to their customer-centricity. As a result, they enjoy significant benefits.

Finally, how to build a Touchpoint Structure

So why aren't more companies customer-centric? The answer is relatively simple – they either haven't realized that they need an Experience Strategy and Touchpoint Structure, or haven't figured out how to establish one or both. I wrote *TOUCHPOiNT POWER* to share exactly *how* to develop an Experience Strategy, and *how* to build aTouchpoint Structure that serves the Strategy.

In *TOUCHPOiNT POWER* you will learn a proven model and innovative secrets – turning yourself, your group or department, organization or enterprise into a dynamo of consistently customer-centric touchpoints.

Good news and really good news

The fact that so few organizations are truly customer-centric works in your favor. The good news is that achieving a customer-centric culture is hard, and as a result, is achieved by very few organizations. The really good news is that once achieved, you will enjoy a long-term and defendable competitive advantage. Unlike the differentiators of quality/innovation or price, customer-centricity is a differentiator that can't be bought.

As a Customer Centric Organization

Your customers and employees will love you and sing your praises, your competitors will envy you and grumble about how you get all the breaks, and you will reap the rewards of having built a defensible competitive advantage that drives growth and profitability.

The information in *TOUCHPOiNT POWER* provides you with a choice:

- Slug it out on price (good luck)
- Keep trying to out-quality/innovate your competitors and hope
    - Your customers can actually tell the difference
    - Your customers recognize enough difference/value to pay the premium this differentiator requires
    - Your competitors don't care enough, or can't afford to pay to catch up
- Or, apply the lessons of *TOUCHPOiNT POWER* to build a Touchpoint Structure, become customer-centric and seize a defendable competitive advantage and leadership position in this new Touchpoint Economy

Competition is also focusing on differentiating through Customer Experience

If your organization hasn't realized the opportunity to differentiate through customer experience, your competition probably has. This Forrester research shows that those organizations with customer experience professionals are seeking to build customer experience as their differentiator.

9

FORRESTER April 2012 "The State Of Customer Experience, 2012 "
Three-Quarters Of Respondents Hope To Use Customer Experience As A Differentiator

"How would you describe your executive team's goal for customer experience?"

To differentiate ourselves from all firms across any industry	11%
To differentiate ourselves from competitors in our industry	64%
To maintain parity with other leaders in our industry	7%
To keep from falling too far behind leaders in our industry	2%
To stay in the mainstream in our industry	8%
To stay slightly behind the mainstream in our industry	1%
Our executive team doesn't have explicit goals related to customer experience	6%

75% of respondents said their executives aim to differentiate on the basis of customer experience.

Base: 84 customer experience professionals who know about their executive team's goal for customer experience
(percentages do not total 100 because of rounding)

Source: Q4 2011 Global Customer Experience Peer Research Panel Online Survey

Reprinted with permission

Are your competitors working to build customer-centricity as a differentiator and a competitive advantage against your organization?

There is an upside to customer-centricity

The CFI Group created stock portfolios based on data from the American Customer Satisfaction Index (ACSI) and the National Customer Satisfaction Index UK (NCSI) to compare the relationship between customer satisfaction and financial success. Stocks were bought long or sold short based on satisfaction index performance. A $100 investment in the ACSI fund over two years ending April, 2012 was a gain of 390%. During the same time, the S&P 500 returned a 7% loss. The NCSI portfolio earned a 59% return over a 50 month period ending June, 2001, compared to a London Stock Exchange FTSE loss of 6%.[3]

Preface/Credibility
The evolution of my Touchpoint Structure

As the result of a short career as a professional golfer and experience managing fine dining restaurants, I got into the management of private

---

[3] www.cfigroup.com/downloads/Customer_Satisfactin_and_Stock_Returns_CRI_Group.pdf

golf, country and dining clubs. Due to the high expectations of members, I believe fine private clubs represent one of the most demanding customer experience environments. I excelled in this environment and it was here that I started to build my touchpoint concepts and structure.

As the new general manager of a country club struggling to retain and attract members, I assessed the situation and surveyed members. I then developed a plan that started with the basics to improve the touchpoints commonly encountered by members and their guests.

Intensive training of the staff improved human touchpoints. The newsletter was updated and professional promotional signs were incorporated to improve communication touchpoints. The interior of the clubhouse was updated to improve physical touchpoints. New menu items utilizing fresher ingredients were instituted to improve sensory touchpoints.

Cover the basics, then add value

With the basics covered, I was then able to move on to touchpoints that added value for our members.

- After the weekend morning tee time rush I had a large golf cart staff with little to do – so I launched a program offering car washing and detailing services
- I found a local dry cleaner that would provide pick up and drop off service and offered dry cleaning service through our locker room staff
- In our fine dining room, we moved to providing glass dome service – each entre served under a dome removed simultaneously by a chorus of staff

Both members and employees loved the new touchpoints. These improvements changed the perception of the club – our Identity – in the minds of our members and staff. The change in perception driven by improved touchpoints served as a key driver in the renaissance of this business. In my three years there, we increased members satisfaction across the board and adjusted net income a whopping 158%.

As the initial incubator of my Touchpoint Structure, the experience at this club helped me realize the power of each touchpoint working together to consistently create a desired Identity, and the financial impact this can have on the organization.

A critical business gap identified

Following my passion for strategic planning, I moved on from club management to launching a strategic planning consultancy. In helping organizations develop their strategic and/or marketing plans, I recognized a critical business gap. I call this the *strategy-to-touchpoint gap*.

Strategy-to-Touchpoint Gap

To realize the full potential of any strategic plan, it must "live" at the touchpoint level. Closing the gap occurs when a structure enables a strategy to be implemented across all relevant touchpoints.

It is relatively easy to develop a strategic plan engaging those at the upper levels of an organization. The challenge is realizing the full potential of a strategic plan. It is tough, some would say impossible, to get a strategy implemented through all levels of the organization such that it is experienced by customers. The truth is, to realize the full potential of any strategy, it must "live" at the touchpoint level. *Closing the strategy-to-touchpoint gap occurs when a structure enables a strategy to be implemented across all relevant touchpoints.*

My work in private clubs and strategic planning formed the foundation for my professional passion – helping organizations improve customer and employee acquisition, satisfaction and retention through closing the strategy-to-touchpoint gap.

While this gap can exist for any strategy, most organizations are missing both an Experience Strategy and a Touchpoint Structure.

Launching a pioneering consultancy and inventing a foundational methodology

Early in 2002, I put together a team of really smart people as part of launching a new research consultancy. The purpose of the consultancy was to help organizations reap the benefits of closing this gap with a focus on improving customer touchpoints.

Understanding that touchpoints serve as the intersection of company and customer, our consultancy built our research and consulting on methods for identifying, evaluating, improving and measuring touchpoints. Every day we focused on helping our clients by advancing our touchpoint based concepts, methodologies and tools.

One key invention was our pioneering process for identifying and mapping individual touchpoints along a single customer's journey. This process of

Touchpoint Path

The touchpoints of a single or typical customer mapped sequentially along their experience or journey.

mapping touchpoints along a single path serves as a foundation for most Customer Experience Management methodologies today.

> Note: Customer Experience Management is typically abbreviated CEM or CXM. In *TOUCHPOiNT POWER* Customer Experience will be abbreviated CX and Customer Experience Management CEM.

Over the years our team applied our methodologies and tools to organizations large and small, including several of the largest companies in the world. For each step of our journey, we were learning, and as a result, improving our efforts and results. I came to recognize a series of critical factors:

- The core problem Customer Experience Management (CEM) must solve
- The three competencies an organization must develop to both address the problem and build a customer-centric culture
- The strategy-to-touchpoint gap and the structure that is missing – the structure that is needed to close the gap.

It was an exciting time as we drank from the fire hose of customer experience knowledge – working around the clock and continually challenged each other on how we could improve. In those early days it was a wild ride and we absolutely loved it.

Over the years I have helped organizations from individual sole proprietors to large multinational organizations, including a number of prominent companies in the Fortune 100. Each of these organizations achieved customer touchpoint improvements that delivered quantifiable increases in financial metrics. I have also had the honor of speaking on four continents on the subjects of Customer Experience Management, Experience Strategy, Touchpoint Structure, Customer Touchpoints and How to Build Customer-Centricity.

Preface/New Discipline
A discipline evolves

When we started the research consultancy this new discipline didn't even have a name. Practically (okay perhaps a bit selfishly), I thought it should be called Customer Touchpoint Management. By the time

13

we sold that consultancy to a Canadian private equity firm, the discipline had evolved to be known as Customer Experience Management (CEM).

Applying expertise in-house

After starting this book and speaking around the world on CEM, I then went in-house to apply my CEM knowledge to building a customer-centric culture for a global operating company of a Fortune 50 conglomerate. Using the techniques revealed in this book, my team helped improve "likelihood to recommend" 15 points in 18 months.

A $37,500,000 impact

Perhaps more importantly, I was able to correlate that a one point improvement in "likelihood to recommend" resulted in a $2.5 million increase in top-line revenue for that organization. The 15 point improvement achieved over 18 months correlated directly to an annual increase in revenue of $37.5 million. My original formula for calculating the impact on revenue of a one point movement in "likelihood to recommend" can be found in the Resources Section and is Doc # 500, Brigman's CX Correlation Formula™, *www.TouchpointPower.com/members*.

The above is a brief summary of some of the experiences, expertise and tools I bring to bear to share with you through *TOUCHPOiNT POWER*. It is my hope that you too can reap the benefits for your customers, colleagues and employer.

Preface/Applicability
TOUCHPOiNT POWER is universally applicable

The beauty of the model revealed here is that it is universal and applicable to any type of organization

- Profit or not-for-profit
- Private or public
- Corporate or closely held
- Large or small
- Local, regional, national, multi-national
- Centralized or decentralized
- B2B or B2C or B2G or G2C (business-to-business, customer or government, and government to constituent)

Serving any type of "customer"

- Suspect
- Prospect
- Customer
- Client
- Partner
- Patient
- Donor
- Student
- Constituent
- Vendor
- Channel
- Shareholder
- Owner

Applying any type of process or management philosophy or tool

- Six Sigma
- Lean
- Total Quality Management
- Management by Objectives
- Balanced Scorecard

Covering any level of scope

- Personal
- Group
- Function
- Department
- Enterprise
- Culture

In whatever job you hold

- Customer-facing
- Support
- Operations

- Management
- Executive

Customize to your needs

While *TOUCHPOiNT POWER* will serve organizations of any size, it is primarily written from the large organization perspective. If your organization or department is small, adjust the scope of the ideas as needed to meet your situation and needs.

TOUCHPOiNT POWER will serve as your guide whether you want to improve your own personal customer interactions, or those with or within your department, or if you want to improve the culture of your multinational enterprise.

I have written *TOUCHPOiNT POWER* as a guide for how to differentiate and establish a defendable competitive advantage through an "Experience Strategy" focused on building a customer-centric culture. If your strategy is less ambitious, and that is certainly understandable, you can scale back the methodologies and tools as needed to accomplish your strategy. You can also start by simply applying some of the methodologies and tools to address specific customer experiences or low-hanging fruit. If desired, more ambitious goals can certainly follow successful tests or pilots. In the closing chapter, I explore options for exactly where and how to start under different scenarios.

Preface/*TOUCHPOiNT POWER* Is & Isn't

TOUCHPOiNT POWER is...

This is a Customer Experience Management how-to guide that will help you achieve your customer experience goals.

TOUCHPOiNT POWER isn't...

Through *TOUCHPOiNT POWER* I am not going to spend a great deal of time and space trying to convince you that Customer Experience Management (CEM) is good business. The fact that you are reading this indicates you have an appreciation for, and interest in, improving customer-centricity. Rather than spend hundreds of pages waxing on about why it is important and valuable to improve customer-centricity – there are plenty of books and research that cover that topic – let's save paper and time and just agree that, conceptually, improving customer-centricity makes sense and that it is good business.

Laser focused on "how"

While I will use short antidotes and stories to improve your understanding of presented concepts, my focus is that after reading *TOUCHPOiNT POWER* you will know exactly:

> *How to get and keep more customers by developing, implementing and measuring a compelling Experience Strategy through building three critical competencies and a structure to get the Strategy and competencies to live across each touchpoint.*

Preface/Sections

Four powerful sections

TOUCHPOiNT POWER is formatted in four sections. The first three sections open with a story regarding the power of touchpoints and are broken into chapters, each ending with a summary of key points. The last is a section of resources.

As with all disciplines, Customer Experience Management (CEM) has its own language. Think of the words associated with the disciplines of accounting or marketing. CEM is no different. As a result, there may be a number of terms included and introduced in *TOUCHPOiNT POWER* that are new to you. Definitions of many terms are provided in the text or call-outs. If a source is not provided, it is an original definition. A complimentary CEM e-Dictionary of words and acronyms used in *TOUCHPOiNT POWER* is available for download at *www.Touchpoint-Power.com/resources.*

Following this Preface, you will find **Section I, Customer Experience (CX).** In Chapter 1 the core experience problem is identified along with the ways in which organizations perpetuate the core problem. An analogy is drawn between product and customer journeys. This analogy helps frame the purpose of CEM and the value of building the Touchpoint Structure found in iconic customer-centric organizations and missing in most other organizations.

Chapter 2 introduces the solution and key foundational concepts along with a hierarchy of terms. With this knowledge, we become clear on the task we must undertake to reap the benefits of addressing the problem.

In Section II, **The Three Competencies of a Customer-Centric Organization** is a deep dive into the competencies your organization must build in order to become customer-centric.

This section includes separate chapters for each of the Three Customer-Centricity Competencies™ - Identity, Intelligence and Consistency.

Section III, **How To Build Customer-Centricity** details how to build the Three Competencies and Touchpoint Structure to achieve customer-centricity and get and keep more customers.

Each step of a presented four-step model serves as a building block. It is truly a step-by-step guide and a differentiator for *TOUCHPOiNT POWER* versus most books on the subject. This section also includes a relevant case study. With an integral understanding of the model, you can adapt and customize it to your unique situation.

The last chapter of this section is a summary that includes success secrets and recommended first steps. These first steps are framed within the context of starting big, with the support and resources needed, or starting smart and having to build consensus that CEM is the right organizational focus. Implementation for small businesses is also discussed.

TOUCHPOiNT POWER also includes a **Resources** Section. Here you will find my touchpoint naming convention and a formula for correlating a one point movement in Net Promoter®[4] score to top-line revenue. Samples of many of the forms and tools mentioned in *TOUCHPOiNT POWER* are available for free downloaded at *www.TouchpointPower.com/Resources*. There you can also learn about the *TOUCHPOiNT POWER* Toolbox, which includes interactive versions of the forms and tools, and a thorough workbook.

Preface/Layout
A layout geared to your needs

TOUCHPOiNT POWER is organized in a way to allow you to consume the information you need as efficiently as possible.

Paragraph or section headers provide insight into the content that follows. As concepts are introduced, a brief definition or description is provided in the main text and/or in a callout.

---

[4] Net Promoter® and NPS® are registered trademarks of Bain & Company, Inc., Fred Reichheld and Satmetrix Systems, Inc.

Deep Dives provide detail and context

Detailed explanations or examples of some concepts are presented as "Deep Dives." Deep Dives are shaded and can be read as a continuation of the book, or, you can choose to skip those Deep Dives that aren't as relevant to your situation or where you are already well versed. It is up to you.

Rants for opinions and to challenge convention

Another type of Deep Dive is a "Rant." I even offer Mini Rants. For Rants, I go off on a topic providing a deeply held personal opinion – no supporting documentation required. Agree or disagree – my hope is that the included Rants prompt you to think.

Breadcrumb for location and reference

Like the breadcrumb of a web page, TOUCHPOiNT POWER provides you with a breadcrumb to help you understand where you are in the book. Grayed out, the breadcrumb convention is: **Section/Chapter/ Topic/Sub-topic.**

"Customer" and "product" applied as ubiquitous terms

As you dive in, you should be aware of how I will be applying a couple of terms. First, the term "customer" in this book is universal and applies to prospects, customers, clients, patients, donors, constituents, students, partners, shareholders, vendors, etc. Second, the term "product" applies to both products and services.

Truths, Rules and Secrets

As you read along you will come across the Truths, Rules and Secrets I share to provide context.

Truths: Those theories I hold to be absolute.

Rules: Important regulations to apply to your CEM efforts to improve the probability of success.

Secrets: Tips and tricks I have learned along my CEM efforts to improve results.

PowerPoint deck you can use

Most of the images in *TOUCHPOiNT POWER* are done in PowerPoint. Many of these PowerPoint slides can be downloaded as a PDF presentation from *www.TouchpointPower.com/resources*. There you will find both a full version of a presentation as well as a condensed deck that is more representative of an executive summary. These slides can be helpful to introduce the concepts of *TOUCHPOiNT POWER* to colleagues, managers, executives and boards.

Preface/Additional Resources

The enormous amount of time, effort and energy I have invested in producing *TOUCHPOiNT POWER* has been a labor of love. This is written as a stand-alone how-to guide complete with methodologies, exercises, a valuable formula and examples of tools and forms. This book, along with the related complimentary PowerPoint slides and resources on my web sites, *www.TouchpointGuru.com* and *www.TouchpointPower.com*, are designed to serve as your Customer Experience Management field guide.

I recognize that there will be readers who will want additional resources and/or services and I have produced a line of products and services to meet that need. These products and services include the *TOUCHPOiNT POWER* Toolbox™, TOUCHPOiNT Ware™, my speaking and coaching services, and Customer Experience Strategies, Inc., the consultancy I founded. Where relevant in *TOUCHPOiNT POWER*, these offerings may be referenced.

For those not interested in any additional products or services, please disregard the references and information. Whether you are interested in additional resources or not, I am confident that you will find enormous value in this book and related complimentary resources.

Preface/Upside
A huge upside

Upon completion, you will have the understanding and tools to develop and implement your Experience Strategy and build your Three Customer-Centric Competencies to the point of establishing a defendable competitive advantage.

A stake in the ground for improvement and discussion

Improving customer-centricity is a dynamic process that requires creativity and dedication. It is my hope that *TOUCHPOiNT POWER* not only helps you in your efforts to improve customer touchpoints, experiences and loyalty, but that it also advances the discussions and discipline of Customer Experience Management.

Use, modify and apply as you deem appropriate for your situation.

Read. Create. Apply. Benefit.
Enjoy!

Preface/Summary
Key Points

- Touchpoints are powerful

- Three differentiation options are:

    □ Quality/innovation

    □ Price

    □ Service/experience

- Entering the new Touchpoint Economy

- Three results of a touchpoint – your customer can:

    □ Say something good

    □ Say something bad

    □ Say nothing at all

- Organizations are often missing an Experience Strategy and a Touchpoint Structure

- The strategy-to-touchpoint gap must be closed to maximize the impact of any strategy, and especially to become customer-centric

- Good news and really good news. The good news is that it is hard to become customer-centric – it is so hard that few organizations achieve the cultural shift. The better news is that, once achieved, customer-centricity provides a defendable competitive advantage.

- *TOUCHPOiNT POWER* is a how-to guide applicable to any type of organization

SECTION I

CUSTOMER EXPERIENCE (CX)

The Core Customer Experience

Problem and its Solution

SECTION I

CUSTOMER EXPERIENCE (CX)

As a result of reading this section you will understand key customer experience (CX) principles on which the solutions provided in *TOUCH-POiNT POWER* are based.

In the first chapter, The Problem, the core customer experience problem is introduced. You will gain insights into the four ways organizations perpetuate this problem and the assets two critical journeys create. The Problem Chain that results from the core customer experience problem is defined.

In the second chapter, The Solution, you will gain an understanding of the fundamentals of Customer Experience Management (CEM) and how it solves the core experience problem. This quick course in the new discipline of CEM covers:

- The symptoms that indicate CEM is needed
- The foundations that need to be in place to maximize success
- A nomenclature hierarchy to get everyone speaking the same language
- The three types of customer journeys and their components

The knowledge gleaned from this section is foundational to the information in Section II, The Three Competencies of Customer-Centricity.

CHAPTER 1:
THE PROBLEM

The Core Customer Experience Problem and
How Organizations Perpetuate this Problem

CX/The Power of Touchpoints

Two survey responses lead to a customer experience epiphany

My team and I were administering a survey to all of the employees of a financial services division of a Fortune Five conglomerate. We were engaged to help the organization improve its customer-centricity. One of the survey's questions was, "What are your personal customer touchpoint best practices – what do you do that is especially customer-centric?" Little did I know that two answers to this one question would produce an epiphany.

Am I waiting two hours or two days?

Most employees in this financial service company were customer facing. A number of them replied to the survey question with how quickly they returned customer phone calls. Sally's response to the best practice question was that she returned all customer calls within two hours. While Sally answered that she returned all customer calls within *two hours,* Samuel volunteered that his customer service best practice was to return all customer calls within *two days!* Remember, Samuel wasn't asked how quickly he returned customer calls, he was asked to identify his customer service best practices.

A customer leaving a voice mail message with both employees could get a return call from Sally in 1 ½ hours and from Samuel in 47 hours. From the customer's perspective, these two responses are *inconsistent*. Yet, both employees *think* that they are delivering a best practice!

CX/Core Problem
Inconsistency is the core experience problem

The contrast between Sally's and Samuel's response prompted my epiphany – the core customer experience problem is inconsistency.

Wouldn't you consider a return call within two hours a pretty positive experience by the company? What would you think if on another occasion your message isn't returned for two days? It is confusing. What should you expect and which company is it – a company where employees return calls in two hours or two days?

> **Core Problem**
> The core customer experience problem is inconsistency

Truth: From both the customer's and organization's perspective, the core customer experience problem is inconsistency.

Getting a call back in two days can make a customer feel like the business just doesn't care. Interestingly, a Rockefeller Corporation study into why customers stop doing business with companies found that 68% leave because they feel that the company doesn't care about them.

If fact, according to the study, customers leave because:

- 1% die
- 3% move
- 5% stop using the product or service
- 9% move to competitors
- 14% are dissatisfied
- 68% feel that the company doesn't care about them

In other words, 82% of customers stop doing business with a company as a result of unsatisfactory or uncaring touchpoints.

The above is consistent with a study commissioned in 2011 by Right-Now Technologies (now Oracle). The Customer Experience Impact

Report conducted by Harris Interaction uncovered:

- 86% of customers stopped doing business as the result of a bad experience
- 26% of those posted negative comments on a social network
- 79% of those complaints were ignored by the targeted companies
- 89% of customers began doing business with a competitor following a poor customer experience
- The #1 reason for recommending a company was outstanding service

Organizations need a structure at the touchpoint level to reverse the negative impact of the inconsistency that perpetuates the unsatisfactory or uncaring touchpoints customers encounter.

CX/Core Problem/Perpetuation
Organizations perpetuate inconsistency

An interesting factor is that most of our organizations actually perpetuate inconsistent touchpoints. To better understand how we do this, let's first look at two journeys that create assets – the product journey and the customer journey.

Product journeys create defined assets

Most manufacturing processes have multiple steps to produce a part or end product. For the typical product journey: There is a design with specifications and a multi-step process that is laser-focused on producing an asset as per the specifications. Employees involved understand the process, specifications and the asset it produces. And the organization understands the value of that asset to the business.

Each step of the product journey works in sequence and in conjunction with previous steps to maintain quality, reduce waste, and produce a viable end product that meets specifications within established quality standards. Along the process, if a part or product deviates from established standards, it is discarded. *The output of this journey is an asset that meets the specifications as designed.*

The steps of a generic product journey might be:

Mold ⇨ Inject ⇨ Demold ⇨ Cool ⇨ Package ⇨ Asset: Product

29

As a department, manufacturing works hard to improve the efficiency of the process that delivers the product asset. And the organization works hard to maximize the value of that physical asset. There is typically a clear organizational focus on deriving maximum value from each and every product it produces.

> Note: Whether or not your organization produces or sells a product, the nature of this manufacturing process is applicable. If yours is a services only organization, think in terms of the steps taken to deliver your primary service. The resultant asset is the defined deliverable or results produced by your service.

Customer journey also creates an asset

Just as the product journey creates an asset, so too does the customer journey. As an example, let's look at a typical business-to-business (B2B) customer journey:

Where the product journey creates a physical asset, the customer journey creates a *perceptual* asset. The asset is the perception in the customer's mind – good or bad – of the organization, product/service or brand. Together, these two assets drive your organization's "Identity."

> Note: Identity is synonymous with how some use the word brand.

Truth: Journeys create assets.

How organizations perpetuate the core experience problem

Customers face challenges in their journeys. The truth is that organizations typically perpetuate the core experience problem of touchpoint inconsistency along customer journeys. We do so in four different ways – we are:

1. Ignorant

2. Anonymous

3. Siloed

4. Ambivalent

> *"If you take good care of the customers, they come back. If you take good care of the products, they don't come back."*
>
> Stanley Marcus,
> former President Neiman Marcus

> *"Products are made in the factory, but brands are made in the mind."*
>
> Walter Landor,
> Founder Landor Associates

CX/Core Problem/Perpetuation/Ignorant

1. Ignorant – we don't know what our customers want or need

How can we be customer-centric if we don't know specifically what our customers want or need? I have found this ignorance to be pervasive. Most of the clients that I have worked with believe that they know their customers well. When faced with actual customer input or feedback, they are surprised by aspects of customers' true wants and needs or the lack of value actually delivered.

If you aren't buying the argument that employees, especially leadership, don't know what their customers want, consider the following example.

Through a thorough Value Stream Mapping exercise with several customers, a client discovered just how much they didn't know about what their customers wanted and valued. This company's customers were resellers of their product line.

The executives involved prided themselves as great marketers. They firmly believed that they provided their reseller customers with great service, that the marketing materials used by their field sales team were highly relevant and that the materials and sales aids provided to their resellers were highly valued.

> **Value Stream Mapping**
>
> A lean manufacturing technique used to analyze and design the flow of materials and information required to bring a product or service to a consumer.
>
> *Source: Wikipedia*

A facilitator guided the group of the company's customers and managers through the process of identifying the touchpoints along their typical customer journey. Once identified, the customers rated each touchpoint across importance, value and need for improvement.

What the executives who sat in on the Value Stream Mapping exercise found was that:

- A whopping 52% of their touchpoints were *not contributing value* to customers

31

- Thirteen percent of touchpoints were *important* but *detracting* value. Think about that: Thirteen percent of important touchpoints were so bad that they actually detracted value.

- Eighteen percent of the touchpoints were *important* but *needed to be improved*

- In the end, only 17% of this company's touchpoints were *important and added value*

Touchpoint

Any interaction – physical, communication, human or sensory – with or within your organization

---

The company's executives were shocked.

An often cited research by Bill Price and David Jaffee further highlights the disconnect:

- 96% of senior executives claimed to be "focused" on the customer

- 80% believed that they delivered a "superior experience"

- Yet only 8% of customers gave them a superior rating

Early in Enterprise Rent-a-Car's efforts to improve customer-centricity, branch managers couldn't accurately pick problems identified by customers more than 50% of the time – about the same accuracy as choosing heads or tails of a coin flip.

> Note: Enterprise Rent-a-Car is a great case study of the benefits of committing to building a customer-centric culture. Their efforts to improve customer experiences were a significant factor in the company more than tripling its revenue in ten years as it overtook the industry leader to become the largest rent-a-car company in the U.S.

Truth: Typically, we are ignorant – we don't know our customers as well as we think we do.

CX/Core Problem/Perpetuation/Anonymous
2. Anonymous – who are we?

How can we work to create a perceptual asset if we haven't defined that perceptual asset – our Identity? This anonymity is foundational in our inability to be consistent in the eyes – and minds – of our customers. Conversely, a clearly defined Identity is a characteristic of the iconic customer-centric companies.

You are personally identifiable by your fingerprint - it is unique to you and always the same. Think of each of your touchpoints with your customer as also leaving a fingerprint. Your organization's customer touchpoints should be unique to it and should always leave the same Identity with each and every touchpoint. Is your organization leaving the same unique identifier every time, or is your fingerprint different with each touchpoint – confusing customers as to the Identity of the organization?

Rule: Define your Identity – the desired perceptual asset in the mind of customers.

CX/Core Problem/Perpetuation/Siloed
3. Siloed – it's about ME

Surprise. Companies aren't organized around customer journeys. As they journey, customers are traversing across departments (or individuals in a small business).

Marketing → Sales → Fulfillment → Service → Accounting → Asset: Perception

However, while our customers traverse *across* our organizations in their journey, we are organized *vertically* in silos. Rather than working horizontally along the journey and the touchpoints customers encounter, we typically work up and down vertically within our various departments.

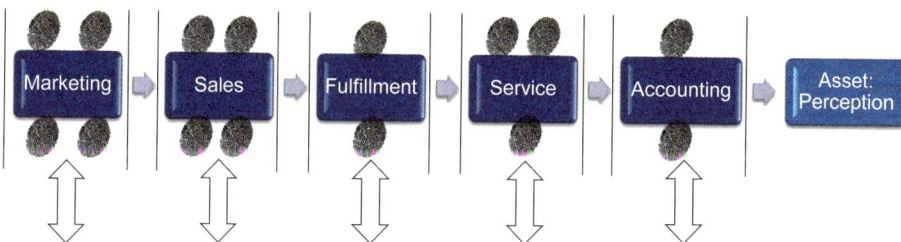

Marketing → Sales → Fulfillment → Service → Accounting → Asset: Perception

Our departments can each have their own budgets, own metrics, own way of doing things. Not only can customers be confused by the independence of each silo, but different silos are often unaware of what other silos are doing. It is not uncommon in large organizations for customer service to get a call from a customer about a sales or marketing program that the customer service rep knows little or nothing about.

33

But how do customers view their journey?

You probably fell right into looking at the customer journey through the steps outlined in the diagram above – a very organization-centric look at the journey. It is easy because these are *our* steps as we deal with customers. But what are *their* steps – what are the stages of the journey from *our* customers' perspective? Customers go through four standard stages up through Selection, and then can progress to various stages in the Post Selection stages (see the Customer Relationship Journey diagram). There is much more on the Customer Relationship Journey in the next section.

A REMiNDER

I often get asked why the "i" in TOUCHPOiNT is small while the rest of the letters are all caps. The reason is to remind me and all of us that our work is about the small "i" and large THEM when developing and deploying customer touchpoints. In working with customers, it is about being, "In THEiR Moment™."

This siloed "me" environment is a major contributor to the core customer experience problem of inconsistent touchpoints. To break it down, we must get better at applying *our* customer journey steps to *their* needs as they progress through the stages of *their* journey.

Secret: Use reminders to ensure that the customer's perspective is front and center.

CX/Core Problem/Perpetuation/Ambivalent
4. Ambivalent – performance left to individuals

Lastly, we perpetuate inconsistency by often leaving performance to individual employees. We apply structure, rigor, systems and metrics to ensure that we churn out products with few defects. We then allow employees to determine how they are going to serve one of the assets we work so hard to acquire – customers. This ambivalence driven inconsistency is how we get employees thinking that it is a best practice to return a customer's call in two days.

CX/Core Problem/Perpetuation/Problem Chain

It all adds up to fragmented and inconsistent touchpoints

Customers must deal with the fact that we may not have a clue as to what they want, haven't defined who we are (our Identity), are actually organized in conflict with how they interact with us and leave the standard of performance of many touchpoints to individual employees.

As a result, for many customers, their journeys are fragmented and inconsistent. Does this sound familiar to you as a customer of the companies you patronize? Chances are, it is the same or similar for the customers of your organization.

Inconsistency is the first domino to fall

The result is the Inconsistency Problem Chain™. The core experience problem of inconsistent touchpoints has ramifications. It is the first domino that starts a chain reaction that dramatically and negatively impacts business, including our purpose.

"The purpose of business is to get and keep customers."
Peter Drucker

Inconsistency Problem Chain™

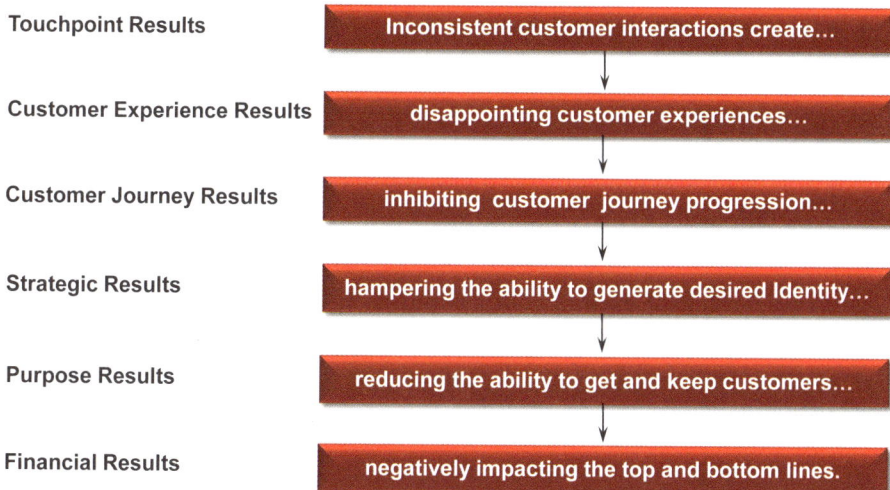

Touchpoint Results	Inconsistent customer interactions create…
Customer Experience Results	disappointing customer experiences…
Customer Journey Results	inhibiting customer journey progression…
Strategic Results	hampering the ability to generate desired Identity…
Purpose Results	reducing the ability to get and keep customers…
Financial Results	negatively impacting the top and bottom lines.

Inconsistent touchpoints negatively impact experiences, which impact the journeys customers have with the organization, which impact the perception of the brand/offering and the purpose of business, getting and keeping customers. This negatively impacts financial metrics.

CX/Core Problem/Symptoms
Symptoms appear everywhere
So how do you know if your customers are experiencing inconsistent touchpoints? Depending on your industry or market, symptoms can include any or all of the following:

- **Stagnate or declining customer metrics**
  - ☐ Customer satisfaction (CSAT)
  - ☐ Loyalty/retention
  - ☐ Net Promoter score (NPS)
  - ☐ Market share
  - ☐ Prospect closing rate (increasing acquisition costs)
  - ☐ Revenue per customer/year
  - ☐ Lifetime customer value

- **Stagnate or declining employee metrics**
  - ☐ Productivity
  - ☐ Satisfaction
  - ☐ Loyalty/retention
  - ☐ Internal Net Promoter score
  - ☐ Accepted offers

- **Stagnate or declining financial metrics**
  - ☐ Margin
  - ☐ Revenue
  - ☐ Profit
  - ☐ Market share

- **Lack of clarity regarding Identity and/or key foundations**
  - ☐ Values
  - ☐ Vision
  - ☐ Mission
  - ☐ Experience Strategy
  - ☐ Experience Position

◻ Differentiation

◻ Value proposition

▪ Performance challenges

◻ Inconsistent employee performance

◻ Increasing customer complaints

◻ Decreasing customer complaints covering issues that have not been addressed but previously had high rates of complaints (customers have given up complaining)

◻ Silo mentality – departments along customer journeys not working well together and pointing fingers at each other

◻ Lack of relevant, timely and actionable data covering customer experiences and/or voice of customer (VOC)

▪ Lack of quantifiable, timely and actionable Customer Experience metrics

◻ Not knowing the negative impact of one or more service issues or policies that trail competitors

◻ Not knowing or having a macro relationship metric, e.g. Net Promoter score, customer satisfaction (CSAT), American Customer Satisfaction Index, Forrester's Customer Experience Index, Temkin Loyalty Ratings, etc.

◻ Not knowing the correlation of your macro metric to a financial metric

◻ Not knowing the performance of key customer touchpoints – lacking transactional metrics and/or the drivers of the macro relationship metric

◻ Not knowing the return on investment (ROI) of your customer experience efforts

So what's *not* included in the list? There is little your organization does that doesn't trickle down to your customers.

Truth: The core experience problem is a big problem in need of a big solution.

CX/Summary
Key Points

- The core customer experience problem is inconsistency
- 82% of customers stop doing business with a company as a result of unsatisfactory or uncaring touchpoints
- Two journeys should create important assets and an Identity
  - Product journey creates a physical asset
  - Customer journey creates a perceptual asset in the mind of the customer
  - Together these assets drive the organization's Identity
- Organizations perpetuate the problem of inconsistency by being
  - Ignorant: We don't know what our customers really want or need
  - Anonymous: We haven't defined our Identity
  - Siloed: We focus on our departments rather than the customer journey
  - Ambivalent: We leave the standard of performance at many touchpoints to individual employees
- An organization's customer touchpoints should be like a fingerprint – always leaving the same and unique Identity
- "The purpose of business is to get and keep customers." Peter Drucker
- The Core Customer Experience Problem of inconsistency creates an Inconsistency Problem Chain
- Stagnate or declining customer, employee, or financial metrics are some of the symptoms of poor customer experiences

CHAPTER 2:
THE SOLUTION

Customer Experience Management (CEM)
and its Foundations

To your customers, you *are* your Touchpoints

Solution/The Power of Touchpoints

It's all about Touchpoints – but what the &%#@ are they?

David Carroll, an unassuming Canadian musician, was sitting in the back of the United Airlines plane as he and his band mates waited to deplane in Chicago to catch a connecting flight to Omaha. Suddenly, a woman screeched, "Oh my gosh, they're throwing guitars."

Carroll looked out the windows and felt the horror in the pit of his stomach as baggage handlers tossed his guitar case around like a football.

In baggage claim, Carroll waited anxiously as he watched bags go around and around. Finally, his guitar case appeared. He set it down, flipped the latches, and opened the sticker covered lid. His worst fears were realized: The baggage handlers had broken his beloved Taylor guitar.

Like most guitar players, his favorite guitar was personal, very personal. It was beloved not because of its cost, but because it had faithfully served as Carroll's main guitar for ten years. He loved its sound. The songs he had written and performed on it held deep meaning to him.

39

No satisfaction from customer service

Thus began a long odyssey over a bad United Airlines touchpoint. For months Carroll attempted to get United Airlines to do the right thing. He told them that he was willing to settle for the repair bill he paid, even though his Taylor didn't sound quite the same.

But alas, United wasn't budging. They were "sorry" about what happened, but were not going to reimburse Carroll for his loss at the hands of their baggage handlers.

Carroll told United exactly what he was going to do. United's negative customer touchpoints prompted Dave Carroll to contemplate his own touchpoint. As a song writer, Carroll decided to do what song writers do – write a song about his experience.

United didn't flinch when Carroll told them that he was going to write a song and post it on YouTube. He also warned United that once the song was posted, he would not accept compensation. United didn't seem to understand the power that customers now have with their own social media touchpoints.

Today, United has a much better understanding of that power. Carroll's first song, "United Breaks Guitars" was posted in July of 2009 (*http://www.youtube.com/watch?v=5YGc4zOqozo*). The lyrics and funny video retell the story of how United Airlines broke his Taylor guitar and refused to remedy the situation. That video on YouTube has exceeded 11,000,000 views and counting. Yes, that's over eleven million times people have viewed this touchpoint about how United Airlines breaks guitars and then doesn't do the right thing.

United now better understands the power of touchpoints

Four days after Carroll posted the music video on YouTube, it had 500,000 views. Did this have an impact on United Airline's stock value dropping 10% or $180,000,000? While direct correlation cannot be verified, it is possible that Carroll's YouTube touchpoint actually had an impact on United's stock price.

Carroll followed the first song with a video statement and two additional songs. YouTube has not been his only communication vehicle for his negative experience. He has also shared the story on several television shows including "The View" and "The Early Show" on CBS. The story has also been told on news programs such as CNN's "Situation

Room." It is also a Harvard Business School case study and Carroll has written a book about the experience. It is estimated that over 150 million people are now aware of this story.

In an effort to make the best out of this public relations disaster, United calls these touchpoints a "learning experience." United is purportedly now using the experience as a part of their customer service training.

Despite United Airlines' efforts after the video was posted to compensate Carroll, he stayed true to his word to not accept compensation once he published his songs. Instead, Carroll asked that United donate the money for the guitar's repair to charity.

Carroll a recipient of complaints regarding United's touchpoints

Based on the email messages Carroll receives, you can't tell that United has learned much from this experience or the subsequent training. It appears as though there are others none too happy with United. Many of these dissatisfied flyers seem compelled to share their story with Carroll.

Solution/Poor Touchpoints
Poor touchpoints impact all types of organizations

Like David Carroll's example, too many customer touchpoints and experiences just plain stink. As customers, we all too often experience indifferent, uninspired and even indignant or insulting service from all types of organizations. When there is a good employee with a good service attitude, they are often working within unwieldy systems that can hinder, frustrate, and even block their customer-centric efforts.

The negative impact of poor customer experiences is not limited by organizational structure or location. Profit, not-for-profit, local, foreign, private, public, B2B (business-to-business), retail and even government can be negatively impacted by poor customer experiences.

Governments taking action

Years ago the web site of Megion, Siberia, quoted its mayor at the time as saying, "Town officials must work out mechanisms to solve and remove problems, not to avoid them." He ordered city employees to stop using certain phrases such as, "I don't know," "I can't," "There is no money," "It's not my job," among others. Those city employees who disobey the ban "will near the moment of their departure."

Recognizing the impact experiences can have on tourism and service industry job growth, Singapore took things further. Years ago Singapore launched an extensive government initiative called Go-the-Extra-Mile-for-Service (GEMS). The stated purpose of this national movement is "to raise service levels and develop a culture of service excellence" to address both economic and social opportunities. The GEMS movement engages service workers, management, and even customers. Four specific areas are identified for improvement – service leadership, service capabilities, service mindset and raising service standards in small & medium-sized enterprises (SMEs).

Singapore's Customer Satisfaction Index improved 1.4% in three years. According to a 2009 National University of Singapore impact study, participating retail and food and beverage organizations have shown a 45% increase in sales growth over their counterparts[5].

Look at how you respond as a customer

Ah, if only we had the power over employees that some government entities appear to have. Of course, not all organizations deliver poor customer experiences. As a customer, you have good and bad experiences and respond accordingly. Chances are you reward with your patronage those organizations that consistently provide positive and rewarding experiences. If they excel, they can earn your loyalty and potentially your advocacy. On the other hand, you know those businesses you avoid, if you can, and the experiences that caused your defection. And you probably told a bunch of people about your dissatisfaction. Perhaps you even wrote a song about it and posted it on YouTube.

Solution/Poor Touchpoints/Solution
A big solution for a big problem

The core experience problem and its symptoms are damaging. To solve these big problems, we need a big solution that addresses the ways in which we perpetuate the core experience problem of inconsistency and allows us to reap the significant benefits of customer-centricity.

The need for a big solution has resulted in the evolution of a new discipline – Customer Experience Management (CEM). CEM is a discipline

---

[5] Source: http://sbr.com.sg/professional-services/news/your-service-government-allots-84m-boost-service-excellence

just like marketing, accounting, sales and finance are disciplines. A difference is that CEM is so new that you probably didn't take a CEM class or get a CEM degree.

To my knowledge, Bernd Schmitt was the first to offer a definition of Customer Experience Management (CEM). In 2003, he defined CEM as, "Strategically managing the customer's entire experience with your product or company."

Today, my Customer Experience Management definition is:

> *The discipline used to comprehensively manage a customer's journeys with your organization, product, brand or service in the efficient creation of value for both customer and organization.*

A discipline to produce a critical asset

For customer journeys to be most successful, each step along the journey should work with the previous step to increase value for both the customer and organization. Each step should reduce waste, and produce the desired end-result asset – your Identity as a perceptual asset in the mind of your customer.

To do so, the customer journey must be viewed and approached in the exact same way as a product journey – it requires a discipline that applies the same rigor and structure. This structure needs to produce a designed output that is a specified asset with everyone working together to produce that asset.

Customer Experience Management

The discipline used to comprehensively manage a customer's journeys with your organization, product, brand or service in the efficient creation of value for both customer and organization.

Changing a focus of your business

Don Peppers or Martha Rogers of Peppers & Rogers gave the closing keynote at several conferences in South America where I delivered the opening keynote. They suggested that organizations change from a product focus to a customer focus – from working to derive and maximize value from products, to working to derive and maximize value from customers – from focusing on the value of the product lifecycle, to focusing on the value of the customer lifecycle. The ultimate shift occurs when the focus changes to actually doing right by the customer. This generates what they call "trustability" in their book, *Extreme Trust: Honesty as a Competitive Advantage* (highly recommended).

43

Truth: The same rigor and discipline applied to maximizing the value of the physical asset produced by the product journey must also be applied to maximizing the value of the perceptual asset of your organization resulting from customer journeys.

Back to United Airlines

Imagine if Captain Denny Flanagan had been the pilot of David Carroll's flight immortalized in the music video, "United Breaks Guitars." As we discovered in the Preface, Captain Flanagan does an extraordinary job. However, are his efforts reflective of United, or Captain Flanagan? In the Wall Street Journal article about Captain Flanagan and his customer-centric ways, Mark Lesser, an advertising executive, notes that, "This guy really came across representing his own standards more than the company's. He's an outlier within United."

Had Denny Flanagan piloted musician David Carroll's flight you could have had two dramatically different perspectives of the same flight. A broken guitar that resulted in a music video blasting the company and seen by millions, and pet owner, frequent first class flyer and father of minor flying alone singing the praise of United and its amazing pilot, Denny Flanagan.

A changed dynamic between customer and provider

Historically, people who encounter bad touchpoints tell several people. But as the United Breaks Guitars example teaches us, the internet and social media have empowered customers and dramatically changed the dynamic between customer and provider. Today, the power of customers and the impact of the touchpoints they encounter and deploy, are greater than ever. Today, a single customer, a single bad touchpoint, can be disproportionally costly to the perpetrating company. And that can be a good thing for customers, a scary learning experience for companies, and costly for owners/stockholders.

Are your prospects able to access reviews of your products/services?

Through the internet and social media customers now have the ability to learn what other customers have found to be the results of their selections and purchases. And a number of recent research efforts uncover that customers have a much deeper trust of the opinions of friends and

fellow customers than they do of advertising and other company-generated marketing.

If you work in the hospitality industry or are a frequent traveler, you are probably well aware of TripAdvisor, the online consolidator of customer reviews of hotels, etc. Most savvy hotels now have a TripAdvisor strategy – it is that important to their business.

Customer reviews of products and services are critical to success. It is so critical that it has spawned a new industry of agencies that help organizations fight bad online reviews. These agencies also typically work to create an improved online image for clients.

Customer Reviews

If your business does not currently face an environment of customer review touchpoints, it soon will. Will your organization be ready for these powerful touchpoints?

Google your company name and "reviews." Also Google your industry or product or service category and "reviews." What appears?

Truth: If your business does not currently face an environment of customer review touchpoints, it soon will. Will your organization be ready for these powerful touchpoints?

Making CEM fit with purpose, foundations and strategy

It is important to understand how CEM efforts ladder up to purpose, foundations and strategies, and how foundations can be used to protect and further CEM efforts.

The purpose of business is to get and keep customers

Peter Drucker

This quote certainly captures the purpose of business and helps to position Customer Experience Management.

Solution/Identity Pyramid™

Deep Dive: Structural Foundations by Any Other Name

What do structural foundations have to do with CEM? This question is at the core of what you want to accomplish. Do you want to address some specific problems and improve targeted customer experiences, or become customer-centric? Becoming customer-centric is a cultural play – it takes place on a foundational level.

45

Different foundations are called different things in different organizations. The key isn't what they are called, but the question they answer.

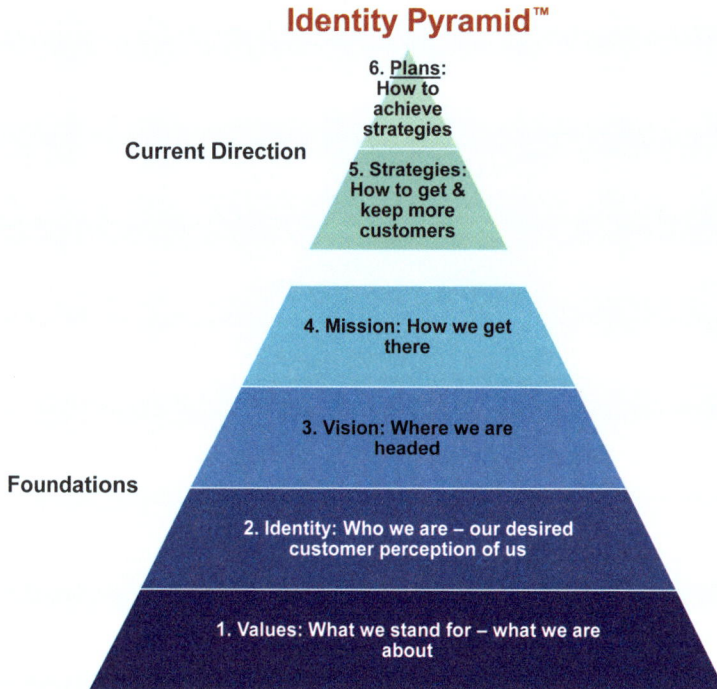

Identity Pyramid™

Current Direction

6. <u>Plans:</u> How to achieve strategies

5. Strategies: How to get & keep more customers

4. Mission: How we get there

3. Vision: Where we are headed

Foundations

2. Identity: Who we are – our desired customer perception of us

1. Values: What we stand for – what we are about

Don't get caught up on whether you have all of these individual pieces. To best achieve our purpose of getting and keeping customers we need foundations, whatever they are called, to address these questions:

1. What do we stand for?

2. Who are we – what is our desired customer perception of us?

3. Where are we headed?

4. How do we get there?

Current direction and objectives build on foundations

To turn these foundations of Values, Identity, Vision and Mission into results, we need strategies and plans – the top of the Identity Pyramid. To get and keep more customers, strategies need to at least cover:

- Operations
- Customer experience

To achieve these strategies, we need plans.

Solution/Identity Pyramid/Foundations/Values

▲ Start with Values

Values are the starting point and represent the building block for all foundations. As we will discuss later, Values can be an asset in defending customer experience (CX) efforts. Values represent what the organizations stands for and what it is all about. Once Values are defined, the remaining foundations can be developed.

As an example, here are the Values of our consultancy. We are:

- **Pioneering.** You will benefit from our thought leadership and practical and innovative methodologies and tools applied with a sense of urgency and attention to detail.

- **A Partner.** You will find us real, striving to understand and to be understood while operating with absolute integrity.

- **Premium.** You will experience great and positive people, touchpoints, solutions and results.

- **Playful.** Together, we will laugh and have fun while accomplishing great things for you, your colleagues, organization, partners, owners and customers.

Solution/Identity Pyramid/Foundations/Identity

▲ Defining your Identity is key

Identity is the perceptual asset we define and seek to create in the mind of customers as they interact with our products and touchpoints along their journeys.

In other words, your Identity is based on the words customers use to describe the organization when someone asks, "Who are they?"

Truth: To be customer-centric, an organization needs to define its Identity and consistently deliver that Identity across all touchpoints.

For our consultancy, we describe ourselves *as passionate hands-on builders working with a sense of urgency.*

We are all about building:

- Consistently customer-centric touchpoints
- Mutually successful, trusting and enduring relationships/ partnerships

47

- Compelling Experience Strategies and comprehensive CEM Plans
- The Three Customer-Centricity Competencies
- Solid Touchpoint Structures
- Cultural change
- Differentiation and long-term competitive advantage
- Loyalty, value and profit
- The discipline of Customer Experience Management

Boiled down, we want to our Identity to be; *hands-on agents of rapid change.*

Solution/Identity Pyramid/Foundations/Vision
▲ Develop a big hairy Vision

Your Vision is a big statement of where your organization is headed. For us, our Vision is to:

Serve the global need to improve the lives of customers, employees & employers

I am fond of really big visions. To me, a vision should articulate something that really captures the spirit of what it is you are aspiring to accomplish on the grandest scale.

Deep Dive: Improving the Lives of Employees

Brenda was one of my favorites at a client's call center. She was a customer service rep who was always happy and wanting to do right by customers – she had a great attitude.

Every day when she sat down in her chair and put on her head set she knew that she was going to get several of "those" calls. You see, her employer had a number of policies that were not all that customer-centric.

This company sold its products to resellers that were mostly small businesses. While they accepted credit cards from the small businesses for purchases, this large, prominent company did not accept the credit card favored by most small businesses. This, despite the fact that its direct competitors did accept the favored card.

This was just the start of the reasons for "those" calls. These small businesses typically placed many orders per week. So what did this large company do?

The company charged these small business owners' credit card each time they ordered. This, despite the fact that its direct competitors charged these small businesses only once per month for their multiple orders.

While these small business owners account for their business on a month by month basis, credit card statements typically don't start from the first and run through the end of the month – they might run from the 12th through the 11th.

Ongoing irate customer calls

As a result, Brenda frequently got "those" calls. Customers irate that her company didn't take the credit card they preferred to use. Customers irate that their other card was charged each time there was an order. Customers irate that it was so hard to reconcile their credit card statement with their monthly accounting. Customers irate that they couldn't pay their account with their credit card over the phone. Brenda and her colleagues have to absorb this negativity daily as part of their job.

Rule: Don't make it hard for customers to pay your organization.

Clueless executives

Brenda and all of the customer service reps had been taking "those" calls *for years* by the time I was brought in. Yet executives of this market leader had *no idea* this was going on.

Imagine working for a company that talks a lot about doing right by customers and employees but isn't even aware of a major problem with one of its policies and *how that policy negatively impacts both customers and employees.*

The disconnect between senior executives and the lives of their front line employees has been highlighted in a television show, *Undercover Boss.* In each episode a chief executive goes undercover as a new hire in a front line position with his or her company. The epiphanies are numerous as these executives actually get to live under the policies and systems of their organization. They not only get to see and feel the negative impact on employees of many of their policies and systems, but also the negative impact on their customers and their business.

While I work hard to improve the lives of customers, I take my greatest satisfaction in improving the professional lives of people like Brenda. It is gratifying when I know that when she sits down in her chair every day she no longer has to fret about receiving "those" calls.

49

Executives – what decisions have you made that force your front-line employees to bear the brunt of restrictive policies and systems and irate customers? Do you even know?

Secret: Want to know where your organization has opportunities to improve customer experiences? Sit with your employees who field customer complaints every day.

Solution/Identity Pyramid/Foundations/Mission
▲ Define your Mission

Your Mission is an overview of *how* you are going to achieve your Vision. For us, our Mission is to:

> *Provide a disciplined approach to building customer-centric cultural change. Apply education, guidance, training, methodologies, tools and structure to expeditiously improve and quantify customer and employee experiences, touchpoint by touchpoint.*

Solution/Identity Pyramid/Current Direction

Foundations are rarely, if ever, changed. To drive the foundations and accommodate ever-changing marketplaces, organizations need strategies and plans that make up their current direction.

Solution/Identity Pyramid/Current Direction/Strategy
▲ Two strategies are key to the purpose of getting and keeping customers

Your strategies are best built on your Identity Pyramid's foundations – they need to serve and advance these foundations.

Maximizing the ability to get and keep customers requires at least two strategies – a Brand/Offering Strategy (sometime called an operational strategy) and an Experience Strategy.

Your organization probably has a clearly defined operational or brand/offering strategy. Initially defined in your business plan and continued in strategic plans, brand/offering strategies typically cover the services or products you offer, how you produce them, where you offer them, how you distribute them, how much they cost, and how and

Brand/Offering Strategy + Experience Strategy = Maximize Purpose

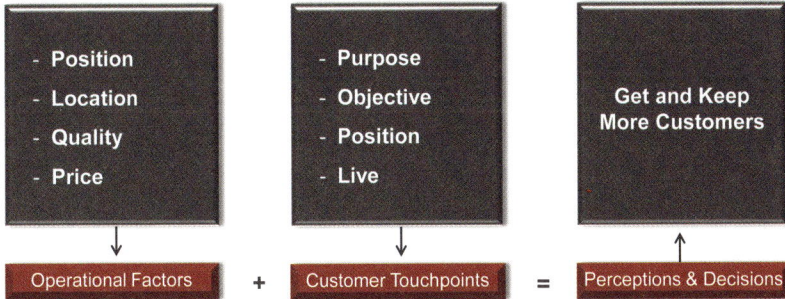

Position - Location - Quality - Price	Purpose - Objective - Position - Live	Get and Keep More Customers

Operational Factors **+** Customer Touchpoints **=** Perceptions & Decisions

where you market, sell, service and account for them. The components of this strategy typically align with the functional organization of your enterprise, such as manufacturing, sales, marketing, etc. *What* is done by an organization and its departments is covered in this strategy.

Experience Strategy is about *how*

Where your Brand/Offering Strategy is about *what* you offer and do, your Experience Strategy is about *how* your customers experience your brand/offering, and what you want to accomplish as a result.

Your Experience Strategy encompasses answering:

1. *Purpose.* *Why* undertake CEM?

2. *Objective.* *What* are the desired results?

3. *Position.* *Where* position:
   a. Customer service policies?
   b. The execution of customer touchpoints?

4. *Live.* *How* do customers experience the organization's Identity?

Experience Strategy helps solve the core problem

A challenge faced by most organizations is that they don't have a comprehensive Experience Strategy. This lack of strategy is a key contributor to the core customer experience problem -— inconsistency.

Rule: To maximize your ability to get and keep customers, establish an Experience Strategy.

Operationalizing your Experience Strategy through CEM

Just as you use the discipline of sales to implement your sales strategy, you use the discipline of CEM to implement your Experience Strategy.

Solution/Identity Pyramid/Current Direction/Plan

▲ Plans deliver strategies

Your Experience Strategy guides the development of your Customer Experience Management Plan and its goals and objectives.

> Note: *TOUCHPOiNT POWER* is written for an Experience Strategy and CEM Plan focused on building a customer-centricity culture that differentiates and establishes a competitive advantage. Your Experience Strategy doesn't have to be as ambitious. Much more on developing an Experience Strategy in the How To Section.

Values, Identity, Vision and Mission are foundational – they make up the bottom of the Pyramid and rarely change. Strategies and the Plans represent the organization's current direction. Found at the top of the Pyramid, Strategies and Plans need to change to serve the needs of the organization in a dynamic market.

Solution/Nomenclature

A new discipline with problems and opportunities...

We are in the early stages of this new discipline of Customer Experience Management (CEM) and practitioners face challenges. At this point, there is a lack of accepted and known nomenclature, methodologies, processes, tools and structure. While there are challenges, this new discipline also creates opportunities as an emerging profession with an insatiable need for talent, especially at the executive level.

...and language

Are terms such as lifecycles, journeys, experiences, steps, processes, interactions, touchpoints, touches, moments of truth and on and on and on used in your company? What does each mean? How are they different? Which ones are synonyms?

As the first to define the word "touchpoint" on Wikipedia, I am always amazed at the various ways in which the word is used, and as a result, its many potential and confusing meanings.

The CEM nomenclature hierarchy starts with journeys.

Solution/Journeys
Understand the different customer journeys

To implement an Experience Strategy and maximize the value of customer journeys, there needs to be an understanding of the three types of customer journeys:

- **Relationship.** The macro journey of universal stages that covers the life of the relationship.

- **Transactional.** Subset of the Relationship Journey that can happen once or repeatedly as the customer goes through the purchase process along a journey that is unique to the organization.

- **Value Add.** Adds value beyond, or in addition to, the product or service. Examples include obtaining education/training, engaging in social networking, attending a special event like a holiday party, etc.

There are Three Types of Customer Journeys
Relationship, Transactional and Value-Add.

Solution/Journeys/Relationship
Customer Relationship Journey is universal

The Customer Relationship Journey (CRJ) is the macro journey. The CRJ consists of seven universal stages. A customer can advance to, stay in, or return to any or all of the stages of the Relationship Journey. The stages are the same whether the customer is selecting a can of soup, a home, an accountant, or enterprise software. The primary difference in a Customer Relationship Journey to purchase a home verses a can of soup is time.

The 7 stages of the Customer Relationship Journey

1. Awareness
2. Knowledge
3. Consideration
4. Selection
5. Satisfaction
6. Loyalty
7. Advocacy

CUSTOMER RELATIONSHIP JOURNEY

GETTING — Awareness, Knowledge, Consideration, Selection
KEEPING — Satisfaction, Loyalty, Advocacy

™ Hank Brigman, www.TouchpointGuru.com

53

Deep Dive:
The Seven Customer Relationship Journey Stages

1. The Awareness Stage

There are two components of the Awareness stage – need/want, and availability. Customers must be aware of a need or want to be filled in order to progress to subsequent stages. To engage with your specific company or product, a potential customer must be aware that your organization can potentially meet their need or want.

Awareness of availability can also come as a result of the next stage – Knowledge. After a need or want surfaces, the prospective customer may enter the Knowledge stage and become "aware" of an organization that can meet the need or want and/or that has availability.

2. The Knowledge Stage

The Knowledge Stage is critical to customer decision-making. This can be a highly dynamic stage of information gathering. Customers may interact with many different types of touchpoints to gain the knowledge or information they seek. The most common Knowledge stage touchpoints include advertisements, product packaging, websites, brochures, white papers, blogs, consumer reviews and other sources of written information as well as referrals from the prospect's circle of influence.

Today, customers can gain vast amounts of knowledge about your organization and its products and services without your awareness. This increases the importance of the touchpoints you develop and deploy to meet or influence Knowledge stage needs.

The duration of the Knowledge stage is typically tied to the importance or sophistication of the selection decision. Gathering information and gaining Knowledge in a grocery store about which can of corn or soup to consider is a process that typically requires far less time and investment of energy than purchasing a home or enterprise software or selecting a building for office space or a store.

Whether selecting the right size of bucket of chicken for dinner or an agency to develop a new go-to-market strategy, the Knowledge stage serves to help create awareness of a prospect's options. The prospect gathers the information needed to determine which options progress to Consideration.

3. The Consideration Stage

The Consideration Stage is where potential customers vet the options they are aware of and that appear to serve their need or want. Customers will weigh these options against their hierarchy of needs.

These three stages, Awareness, Knowledge, and Consideration, can be linear or repeated. The Knowledge stage can bring awareness of new or different options. The Consideration stage can highlight the fact that none of the current options satisfy a prospective customer's needs, returning the prospect to previous stages or prompting them to leave the journey altogether.

4. The Selection Stage

The prospect weighs the options against their hierarchy of needs, and makes a Selection. For some products or services, the Selection stage can be complicated, time consuming and actually not end up with a completed deal. Think about purchasing a home. Making an offer on your chosen house is just the first step. As a part of the Selection stage you submit the offer, which can lead to negotiation back and forth. If a price is agreed upon, there is the whole process that can include appraisal, inspection, securing the loan or loans and closing the deal. This varies dramatically from selecting a can of soup from among the options and promptly paying for it at checkout.

5. The Satisfaction Stage

Once a selection has been made, a customer can become satisfied or dissatisfied. This stage is not so much about product or service performance, but product, service or organizational performance versus expectations.

Expectations of new car owners include that the car will function problem free for quite a while, and if a problem arises, it will be quickly addressed by the dealership. So, while everyone is satisfied with their selection when they leave the dealership, the performance of both the car and the dealership *versus expectations* can, and will, impact satisfaction.

6. The Loyalty Stage

Advancing to the Loyalty stage implies that the customer becomes resistant to competitive options. They are much less likely to be open to competitive marketing messages or to return to a competitive evaluation in the Consideration stage. Instead, loyal customers of repeatable or additional purchases can go directly to Transactional Journeys.

Loyal customers who repeatedly purchase or who make additional purchases are typically highly profitable. The cost to generate additional purchases from a current customer is typically significantly less than the cost to generate a new customer.

Much of customer behavior in the Loyalty Stage is dependent on the nature of loyalty for your organization.

Truth: Loyalty is not the same for all organizations.

An important aspect of loyalty is that it is not the same for all companies. For some, loyalty means the customer only uses your product or service. For others it may mean that your products or services are the offerings of choice, the go-to offerings, or are always given first consideration.

A commercial building developer's loyalty to Tylenol, his preferred pain relief medicine to address his headaches, may be absolute – he doesn't even consider another brand. His loyalty to his preferred lender may not be as absolute. His loyalty to his preferred lender may be that he always goes to them first with his commercial development deals, but based on rates and other factors, may choose another lender for any given development project.

7. The Advocacy Stage

The holy grail of the Relationship Journey is Advocacy. In this stage the customer is not only loyal to your organization or product, but promotes it to others. An advocate's ability to drive prospects into your organization's sales funnel (the "Getting" stages of the Customer Relationship Journey) can be a key to growth, and can become a growth strategy. This source of new customers is almost always the most cost effective as referred prospects are likely predisposed to select your organization or product.

While the benefit of motivating customers to the Advocacy stage is self-evident, not all customers are potential advocates. In my experience I have found that a percentage of customers are not comfortable as advocates. It has less to do with the organization or product, although that can be a factor, and more to do with the nature of the person. Some customers are just not comfortable advocating, referring, or promoting companies, products or services to others.

Truth: Not all loyal customers are potential advocates.

Solution/Journeys/Transactional

Transactional Journeys

Transactional Journeys are a subset of the Customer Relationship Journey. The Transactional Journey is the journey a customer takes each time to consider, select, pay for and consume or use the product or service.

Transactional Journeys can happen once or rarely, such as purchasing a new roof for your home, or repeatedly or often, such as purchasing groceries or gasoline.

Awareness, Knowledge, Consideration and Selection are the Relationship Journey stages that repeat as the Transactional Journey. These Transactional Journeys then impact the post Selection or Keeping stages of the Relationship Journey – Satisfaction, Loyalty and Advocacy.

Transactional Journey stages are unique to your organization

Where the stages of the Relationship Journey are universal, the stages of a Transactional Journey are specific to the organization. A typical or generic business-to-business (B2B) Transaction Journey would cover; marketing, sales and ordering, fulfillment, service and accounting. A typical B2C (business-to-consumer) Transactional Journey would cover; marketing, shop, purchase and use.

Typical B2B Transactional Journey

Market ➡ Sell ➡ Fulfill ➡ Account ➡ Service ➡ Asset: Perception

Typical B2C Transactional Journey

Market ➡ Shop ➡ Purchase ➡ Use ➡ Asset: Perception

Solution/Journeys/Value-Add

Value-Add Journey

This is a journey a customer takes that adds value beyond or in addition to a product or service. Examples include participating in education or training, engaging in a company-developed community or social networking site, attending a special event like a holiday party, etc.

Improving journey efficiency for both customer and company

Do you have a clear understanding of your customers' journeys and their impact on the stages of Satisfaction, Loyalty and Advocacy? Better understanding customer journeys can help your organization improve journey efficiency for both customers and the organization. A key to improving journeys is to understand their components.

Solution/Journeys/Components

What makes up journeys?

Here is the CEM nomenclature hierarchy I use.

Journeys. Each of the three journeys is made up of experiences, which are made up of touchpoints and influenced by factors.

Experiences. A series of touchpoints that combine to make up a step, process or component of one of the three customer journeys: Relationship, Transactional and Value Add.

Touchpoint. Each interaction - communication, physical, human or sensory – with or within your organization.

$$E=MC^2$$

Factors. Non-interactions that influence selection and perceptions. Examples of factors include price, location, selection, etc.

An experience and its touchpoints and factors

As an example, let's take a look at an outside sales rep's sales call for a B2B business from the sale rep's perspective. This is an experience along a customer's journey that can have a number of touchpoints, such as:

- Call to customer to set appointment – communication touchpoint
- Front door of customer's office – physical touchpoint
- Interaction with receptionist upon arrival – human touchpoint
- Music playing in the lobby – sensory touchpoint
- Meeting customer – human touchpoint

- Brochure shown customer – communication touchpoint shown by human touchpoint
- Brochure handled by customer – physical touchpoint
- Price on brochure – factor communicated via a communication touchpoint
- Quote sent via email – communication touchpoint
- Call to discuss quote and take order – communication touchpoint
- Thank you email – communication touchpoint

This series of touchpoints makes up the experience of the sales call in this customer's journey. The experience is made up of the touchpoints and factors listed above. Fulfillment of the order is another experience complete with its own set of touchpoints.

Touchpoints and factors are key drivers

Independently and together factors and touchpoints drive customer decisions and perceptions – including Identity. Touchpoints are often the primary drivers of emotional connections, a key to motivating customers along the Relationship Journey to the stages of Loyalty and Advocacy.

Truth: Clearly define your CEM nomenclature hierarchy or suffer the consequences of confusion and misunderstandings.

Rule: After clearly defining the nomenclature hierarchy, continually educate the organization on the hierarchy and be obsessed with and police its accurate use.

Solution/Summary
Key Points

- A key to successful CEM is answering the questions of the Identity Pyramid
- Two strategies impact the success of efforts to get and keep customers: Brand/Offering (operational) and Experience
- There are three types of customer journeys:
  - *Relationship.* The macro journey of universal stages that covers the life of the relationship.
  - *Transactional.* Subset of the Relationship Journey that can happen once or repeatedly as the customer goes

through the purchase process along a journey that is unique to the organization.

- ☐ **_Value Add._** Adds value beyond, or in addition to, the product or service (i.e. education/training).

- CEM nomenclature hierarchy

  - ☐ **_Customer Journeys._** Relationship, Transactional and Value Add; each made up of individual experiences.

  - ☐ **_Experience._** A step or process of a journey and made up of individual touchpoints.

  - ☐ **_Touchpoint._** Each interaction - physical, communication, human or sensory – with or within your organization.

  - ☐ **_Factor._** A non-touchpoint consideration (i.e. price or location).

- Touchpoints and factors influence perceptions and journey progression

SECTION II.

THE THREE COMPETENCIES OF CUSTOMER-CENTRIC ORGANIZATIONS

A Deep Dive into the Competencies

Your Organization Must Build in

Order to Become Customer-Centric

SECTION II.

THE THREE COMPETENCIES OF CUSTOMER-CENTRIC ORGANIZATIONS

As a result of reading this section you will gain an understanding of the Three Customer-Centricity Competencies™ - Identity, Intelligence and Consistency – and their importance to a solid CEM Plan that solves the core experience problem of inconsistency.

This section is divided into three chapters – one for each of the Three Competencies. An Implementation Model for building these Competencies is detailed in the following section.

Competencies/The Power of Touchpoints
Taking on the big banks

At the time, Molly Katchpole worked two part-time jobs and lived paycheck to paycheck in Washington. She couldn't afford a monthly fee for her debit card and when Bank of America announced a monthly $5 debit card fee, she decided that this frustrating policy deserved a response.

Katchpole started a petition on Change.org, a website for people to solicit signatures through social media. The web site operators saw the petition's potential and reached out to the press. The rest is history.

Media appearances and hundreds of thousands of signatures and later, TV cameras followed Katchpole as she went to close her Bank of America account. In the end, Bank of America, among other banks, rescinded their $5 debit card fee.

Molly wasn't alone in wielding powerful touchpoints against the powerful

Kristen Christian was also frustrated with her bank. It took her four hours on the phone with various representatives to find out what happened to the funds she attempted to transfer from a personal to a business account within Bank of America.

A couple of weeks later, Bank of America instituted policies and fees applicable to those with less than $20,000 in combined accounts. Kristen was troubled that the big banks didn't seem to care about her or the other Americans who bailed them out during the financial crisis.

So Kristen started "Bank Transfer Day." The original idea was to get her friends to take their money out of the big banks and put it in credit unions.

The idea grew to include a few more than her friends. "The event turned into a movement," Christian says, "It's a peaceful boycott of corporate banking started by one citizen."

Analysis by Javelin Strategy & Research pegged the targeted Bank Transfer Day big bank defections at 600,000. Bank of America CEO Brigan T. Moynihan commented that the bank did take a hit. He noted that Bank of America saw a 20% increase in account closings in the fourth quarter (coinciding with bank transfer day).

The big banks' negative policies and customer touchpoints prompted a single customer to take on the financial behemoths. Through a touchpoint on Facebook this single customer rallied 600,000 people to move their money out of big banks.

The power of positive policies and touchpoints built on the Three Customer-Centricity Competencies™ of Identity, Intelligence and Consistency can ensure the customer-centricity that avoids these types of negative policies and customer touchpoints. Perhaps more importantly, customer-centricity

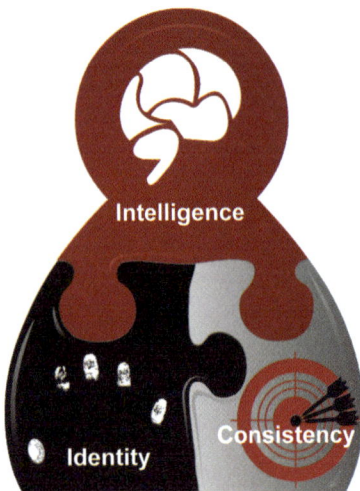

can help avoid the resultant touchpoints of negative customer activism.

Truth: In this new Touchpoint Economy, customer-centricity is the best defense against the power of negative customer-launched touchpoints.

Competencies/Introduction
The Three Customer-Centricity Competencies™

In studying organizations that have solved the core customer experience problem and are recognized as iconic customer-centric organizations, I uncovered what I call the Three Customer-Centricity Competencies™: Identity, Intelligence and Consistency. Companies that have built these Competencies are reaping the growth and profit rewards that accompany differentiating through cultural customer-centricity.

Identity: Define and live your Identity. Customer-centric organizations have clearly defined corporate Values and Identity and incorporate these in all that they do.

Intelligence: Right information to the right people at the right time. Customer-centric organizations generate timely and relevant employee and customer data and feedback. This Intelligence is applied to immediate action, root cause solutions, and planning.

Consistency: Standardize touchpoints. Customer-centric organizations *consistently* deliver touchpoints that meet customer needs and that also reflect their Identity. Consistency is the customer-centricity differentiator as it specifically addresses the core experience problem. It is through building the Consistency Competency that the Touchpoint Structure is established.

These Three Competencies are an output of a Customer Experience Management Plan developed to serve an Experience Strategy geared to achieve customer-centricity.

CHAPTER 3:
THE IDENTITY
COMPETENCY

Define and Live Your Identity

Identity – who you we and what do we stand for?

Your organization's Identity answers the foundational questions: Who are we and what do we stand for?

What happens when these two questions are asked around your organization? Do you get quizzical looks, or the same or similar answers? It is usually one or the other. Either your organization has clearly defined and lives its Identity, or it hasn't defined or doesn't live one.

If your organization is confused as to who it is, where does this leave your customers? A key characteristic of customer-centric companies is that they consistently deliver who they are and what they stand for at each interaction with and within their organization.

What do you think of when...

If I mention the brands Apple, Virgin Atlantic, Disney, Coke or McDonalds, chances are you can quickly voice one or two words that spring to mind for each. That is their Identity to you. The fact that the words you voice would match the words voiced by others for the same company reflects their successful efforts to define and live that Identity – the perceptual asset they created with each and every touchpoint.

So, who is your organization and what does it stand for? Is it innovative, efficient, magical, creative, reliable, green, consistent, refreshing, edgy, customer-focused, progressive, conservative, safe, builders, collaborators, and on and on?

Competencies/Identity/Defining
Who are you?

Defining who your organization is and what it stands for is not an easy undertaking. This can be why so many organizations fail to accomplish this foundational task. Even if accomplished, it is especially challenging to get the organization to actually live the Identity across each and every touchpoint – another example of a strategy-to-touchpoint gap.

Mini Rant: Model Addresses the Gap of the Branding Heyday

Organizations typically hire a branding or advertising agency to lead Identity efforts. These agencies have proven successful at helping organizations define who they are and what they stand for and translating that into a visual mark (logo) and language (messaging). Once the Identity is defined, it is typically quickly applied to marketing communications.

That is the easiest part. A challenge to this practice is that customers encounter many touchpoints that fall outside of marketing communications. What about invoicing, calls into accounting, installation, service, the product itself, sales personnel and on and on?

This is another example of the strategy-to-touchpoint gap. The Identity often lives where it was developed, in the executive suite, and where it is easy to apply, marketing communications. But the Identity most often fails to get introduced or gain traction across non marketing communication touchpoints. This lack of universal adoption hurts or even destroys results – a symptom of the strategy-to-touchpoint gap.

As a result and understandably, many leaders and organizations have become frustrated with "branding." Beyond internal confusion over what the term means or stands for, campaigns have typically failed to meet expectations.

The reason? There wasn't a Touchpoint Structure to incorporate the Identity across every touchpoint – to close the strategy-to-touchpoint gap.

This frustration can be understandable, yet tragic.

Truth: Being able to clearly deliver who you are and what you stand across each touchpoint is foundational for customer-centric organizations.

> Note: in *TOUCHPOiNT POWER*, my references to Identity focus on foundational and experiential aspects. I am not including the visual (logos) and verbal (language) elements typical of most brand/Identity creation and building efforts.

Start with Values

A key to Identity is Values. Organizational Values are often expressed specifically as Values or can be included in a Mission Statement. In whatever form they exist, these Values must be defined, communicated, lived and celebrated in order to become an integral part of the organization's culture. Values are at the base of the Identity Pyramid™.

Identity Pyramid™

Current Direction

6. <u>Plans</u>: How to achieve strategies

5. Strategies: How to get & keep more customers

4. Mission: How we get there

3. Vision: Where we are headed

Foundations

2. Identity: Who we are – our desired customer perception of us

1. Values: What we stand for – what we are about

Iconic companies "live" their Values

Zappos.com values customer engagement such that they don't measure call time. Disney values magical experiences and works to incorporate "magic" across their touchpoints. Apple's value of innovation is reflected in all of their touchpoints and is captured in their "Mission Statement" and "Core Values."

Apple's Core Values:

- We believe that we're on the face of the Earth to make great products.

- We believe in the simple, not the complex.

- We believe that we need to own and control the primary technologies behind the products we make.

- We participate only in markets where we can make a significant contribution.

- We believe in saying no to thousands of projects so that we can really focus on the few that are truly important and meaningful to us.

- We believe in deep collaboration and cross-pollination of our groups, which allow us to innovate in a way that others cannot.

- We don't settle for anything less than excellence in every group in the company, and we have the self-honesty to admit when we're wrong and the courage to change.

Taken from: *http://www.devdaily.com/blog/post/mac-os-x/ apple-busine ss-philosophy-mission-statement/*

These Core Values are the basis for Apple's Mission Statement: *Apple is committed to bringing the best personal computing experience to students, educators, creative professionals and consumers around the world through its innovative hardware, software and Internet offerings.*

There is research that supports the importance of Values and culture to financial success.

Deep Dive:
The Financial Benefits of Building Identity and Values are Real

Excerpt from Richard Barrett's white paper, *Building a Vision-Guided, Values-Driven Organization. Reprinted with permission.*

During the 1990's the average annual shareholder return over a period of ten years was 23% in companies that make up the "100 Best Companies to Work For in America". The average annual shareholder return of the Russell 3000 Index (a general index of American industry) over the same period was only 14%.

In 1998 there were 164 publicly held companies represented in three lists of "best" companies: Fortune Magazine's list of "100 Best Companies to Work For", Industry Week's "100 Best Managed Companies", and Working Mother's list of "100 Best Companies". Of these 164, thirty-eight were on more than one list. These "best" 38 showed consistently superior financial performance over a ten-year period of several percentage points over the 164, and the 164 showed a consistently superior financial performance of several percentage points over the Standards and Poor 500.

In *"Corporate Culture and Performance,"* Kotter and Heskett show that companies with strong adaptive cultures based on shared values outperformed other companies by a significant margin. Over an eleven-year period, companies that emphasized all stakeholders – employees, customers and stockholders, and focused on leadership development, grew four times faster than companies that did not. They also found that these companies had job creation rates seven times higher, had stock prices that grew twelve time faster and profit performance that was 750 times higher than companies that did not have shared values and adaptive cultures.

In *"Built to Last,"* Collins and Porras show that companies that consistently focused on building strong corporate cultures over a period of several decades outperformed companies that did not by a factor of 6 and outperformed the general stock market by a factor of 15.

Develop Identity and Values holistically

Defining your Identity and Values is challenging and should include cross-functional and top to bottom hierarchical representation in addition to customer input. Nothing hurts internal adoption of an Identity more than executives huddled in an ivory tower defining and rolling out an Identity that the rank and file look at as disconnected from their reality. Your Identity has to resonate throughout the organization, while being relevant to customers.

Use the Identity Pyramid as your guide

Answer the questions of the Identity Pyramid and clearly define your Identity. With a clear understanding of your Identity, you have a great foundation on which to build.

Model/Competencies/Identity/Living
What would your janitor say?

Living your Identity involves everyone in the organization from the CEO to the janitors. A great example is the hospital janitor who was asked what he did. The janitor answered, "I help save lives."[6] Think about that. Think about how the janitor's association with the hospital's Identity impacts his approach to his work. Identity can help give employees purpose.

You hire and train to that Identity, and as a result, mirror and model that Identity to the marketplace through your employees. Key contributors to living your Identity include your leader, and those in corporate communications and human resources (HR).

"First, you must decide what you stand for such as "customer service" and then you must align every element of your systems to reinforce that. You must recruit for it, select for it, orient for it, train for it, reward for it, promote for it, and terminate those that don't measure up."

John Young,
Four Seasons Hotels and Resorts

Leaders must model Values to get them to live

Customer-centricity is just like all key efforts – without leadership the effort flounders. While the customer should be experiencing the organization's Values and Identity throughout his or her journeys, the real test lies in whether executives live and enforce them on a daily, ongoing and consistent basis. In my observations, organizations where leaders

---

6 http://www.freibergs.com/resources/articles/leadership/10-things-we-can-learn-from-the-worlds-greatest-surgeon/

consistently reference and live Values and Identity are those where these foundations live much more in the day to day decisions and actions of the rank and file.

Truth: Few things will undermine customer-centric efforts more than a chief executive who doesn't "walk the talk."

The business landscape is riddled with the carnage of organizations whose leaders deviated from their Values or fostered an environment where the Values weren't enforced.

Your people mirror your Identity

Leading by example and celebrating examples of Identity/Values are all geared to impact your employees.

Truth: Your customer touchpoints and experiences are only as good as your employees. Employee engagement is a key component of "living" Identity.

Secret. In business we typically focus on our customers. While customers are a primary focus of *TOUCHPOiNT POWER*, just about everything in this book can also be applied to internal customers – your colleagues and fellow employees.

A partner in helping the organization live its Identity

Human Resources (HR) is a critical partner in getting an Identity to live. It is your HR person or department that typically drives hiring, orienting, training, evaluating, promoting and compensating. Part of living your Identity is partnering with HR to aid their efforts to bake Identity into each of their areas of responsibility.

Capture and celebrate examples of your Identity

Iconic customer-centric organizations know who and what they are about. They continually reinforce that Identity by capturing and celebrating stories that exemplify that Identity. In this way, the Identity becomes self-perpetuating.

Here is a great example of an organization that "lives" its Identity.

Deep Dive: The Ritz-Carlton, an Organization that Gets and Lives Identity

The Ritz-Carlton has clearly captured its Identity in its Credo, Promise and Service Values. To help ensure that the Identity lives, each Ritz-Carlton has a full-time training director. That's right – each property has its own trainer.

Credo

The Ritz-Carlton is a place where the genuine care and comfort of our guest is our highest mission.

We pledge to provide the finest personal service and facilities for our guests who will always enjoy a warm, relaxed, yet refined ambience.

The Ritz-Carlton experience enlivens the senses, instills well-being, and fulfills even the unexpressed wishes and needs of our guests

Brand Identity/Promise

"We are Ladies and Gentlemen serving Ladies and Gentlemen."

Service Values

I am proud to be Ritz-Carlton

1. I build strong relationships and create Ritz-Carlton guests for life.
2. I am always responsive to the expressed and unexpressed wishes and needs of our guests.
3. I am empowered to create unique, memorable and personal experiences for our guests.
4. I understand my role in achieving the Key Success Factors, embracing Community Footprints and creating The Ritz-Carlton Mystique.
5. I continuously seek opportunities to innovate and improve The Ritz-Carlton experience.
6. I own and immediately resolve guest problems.
7. I create a work environment of teamwork and lateral service so that the needs of our guests and each other are met.
8. I have the opportunity to continuously learn and grow.
9. I am involved in the planning of the work that affects me.
10. I am proud of my professional appearance, language, and behavior.
11. I protect the privacy and security of our guests, my fellow employees and the company's confidential information and assets.

12. I am responsible for uncompromising levels of cleanliness and creating a safe and accident-free environment.

Reinforced on an ongoing basis to ensure that they "live"

Each shift has what is called a line-up. The line-up is where managers cover the details of the shift for their area of responsibility. For food servers, this typically involves understanding food or drink specials and what might be 86 (on the menu but not available). For front desk staff, the line-up can cover arriving and departing guests, etc. At each line-up the manager goes over one of the 12 Service Values or stories of how a team member applied one of their Service Values to a touchpoint.

The Ritz-Carlton empowers its employees to deliver its Values (see Service Value #3 above). Each has the ability to commit Ritz-Carlton up to a $2,000 expense in the delivery of one of its Values in the service of one of its guests.

Empowered employees advance the Identity

At a conference, the head of The Ritz-Carlton Learning Center shared this story. A father and his young son were checking into a Ritz-Carlton in New York City, home to Spiderman. The son looked up at the father and asked, "Do you think we will see Spiderman?" Later that day, there was a knock on their hotel room door. Envision the look on that child's face when the door was opened to reveal – Spiderman.

This lifetime memory was provided by a janitor. He overheard the son's question as he did some light cleaning around the front desk when the father and son checked in. Empowered by Ritz-Carlton, this employee contracted with an agency to deliver the Spiderman experience. Wow!

What are your employees empowered to do to advance and live your Identity and wow your customers?

Your organization has an Identity

Whether or not your organization has defined its Identity, it *has* an Identity. Your customers have developed a perception of your organization – good or bad. This image is a direct result of the products/services, touchpoints and factors encountered along your customer's journeys. If your Identity has not been defined, then it will vary touchpoint by touchpoint and customer to customer. This lack of definition erodes the potential value of this perceptual asset.

Competencies/Identity/Summary

Your Identity – the perceptual asset you seek to establish in the minds of your customers – is foundational to your organization's ability to *consistently* deliver positive customer experiences and touchpoints. Defining and living your Identity is a competency of becoming customer-centric.

Key points

Customer-centric organizations work hard to ensure that their customer's perception of them matches their desired Identity.

- They clearly define their Identity and Values
- Their leaders' exhibit and communicate them on an ongoing basis
- Examples of the Identity are captured and celebrated
- Values and Identity are:
    - A basis for hiring and orienting new staff
    - Included in training both new and tenured employees
    - Incorporated in evaluations, promotions and compensation
    - Incorporated into touchpoints
- Whether defined or not, every organization has an Identity

CHAPTER 4:
THE INTELLIGENCE
COMPETENCY

Get the Right Information
to the Right People
at the Right Time

Competencies/Intelligence

To be customer-centric you must know and listen to your customers. While numerous companies engage in aspects of gaining customer Intelligence, few integrate it into immediate action, addressing root cause, and/or planning.

"What gets measured gets done, what gets measured and fed back gets done well, what gets rewarded gets repeated."
John E. Jones, noted experience-based trainer

Competencies/Intelligence/Right Information

Right Information

What does the *right* intelligence look like? There are typically four areas:

- There are "macro metrics" – the primary metrics an organization uses to measure the overall health of customer relationships, and employee teamwork.

Intelligence

- There is correlation – understanding of how movement in the macro customer metric impacts a key financial metric (i.e. top-line revenue).

- Drivers are known – touchpoints and factors along customer journeys that most impact:

  ☐ The macro metrics

  ☐ Journey stage progression, especially to Selection (purchase or repurchase)

  ☐ The Identity - the perception in the customer's mind

- Data is segmented – not all prospects, customers and data are the same. Some are more valuable than others and segmentation can help clarify value.

Competencies/Intelligence/Right Information/Macro Metric

Develop a single relationship metric

Your organization needs a single metric – a macro metric - that provides an indication of the health of your relationship with your customers. A macro metric is: The primary metric an organization uses to measure the health of customer relationships.

Optimally, this metric will be correlated with a financial metric and also be predictive of future performance. There are a number macro metrics from which to choose – Net Promoter score (NPS), American Customer Satisfaction Index, Forrester's Customer Experience Index and Temkin Loyalty Ratings are all examples. Of course, you can develop your own (e.g. Enterprise Rent-a-Car's "Enterprise Service Quality index (ESQi)." For more information on Enterprise's ESQi: *http://aboutus.enterprise.com/customer_service.html*).

Deep Dive: Net Promoter Score (NPS)

While there are critics of all relationship measures, I believe that the advantages of a single relationship metric far outweigh criticisms.

Net Promoter score is one of the most commonly used, and based on a single question:

How likely are you to recommend _____ to a friend or colleague?

Based on a 0 to 10 scale, respondents are classified at Promoters, Passives

or Detractors. The percentage of those that answer as Promoters (9 or 10) minus the percentage of those that answer as Detractors (0 to 6) equals the Net Promoter score (NPS).

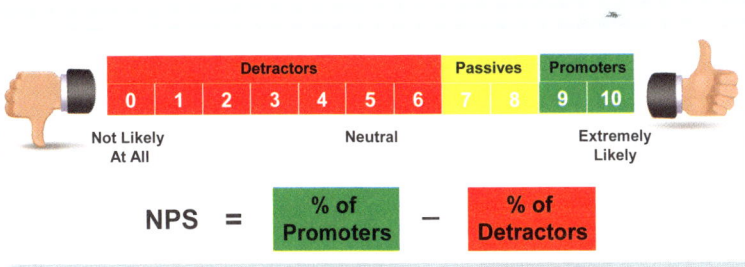

The developer of Net Promoter score, Fred Reichheld, provides the following Rules of Measurement Principles[7]:

- Ask the NPS question and little else
- Choose a scale that works and stick to it
- Aim for high response rates from the right customers
- Report relationship data as frequently as financial data
- The more granular the data, the more accountable the employees
- Audit to ensure accuracy and freedom from bias
- Validate that scores link to behaviors

With NPS, I recommend starting with two questions in addition to your typical segmentation questions (your segmentation questions are critical, especially the ability to tie NPS response to an individual customer).

1. How likely are you to refer a friend or colleague to _____ (insert your company name)?

2. Why (please be specific)?

Choose one, communicate it and understand what drives it

Whatever macro metric you choose or develop, your organization needs to understand its drivers. What makes the macro metric go up or down? This is where the touchpoint data is important. The drivers of your macro metric are typically touchpoints or factors and/or the resultant perceptions of the organization's Identity.

---

[7] Fred Reichheld, The Ultimate Question: Driving Good Profits and True Growth, (2006, the Harvard Business School Publishing Corporation)

Understand segments to deliver appropriate levels of service

Segment information is critical for reasons far beyond customer experience (CX). Within CX, understanding the profitability and growth potential of a segment can help determine appropriate service policies and levels of service. Financial value can be criteria for those organizations that can, or desire to, provide different levels of service for different segments.

How much is a customer worth over their Relationship Journey?

A key metric overall and within segments is Lifetime Customer Value (LCV). Understanding this metric helps an organization focus on what is truly important – increasing the long-term value of each customer.

Truth: The three most powerful tools available to the CX professional to help guide their organization to make customer-centric decisions are:

- Values/Identity
- Financial correlation of the macro customer relationship metric and financial metric(s) (typically top-line revenue)
- Lifetime Customer Value

Mini Rant: Important Assets to Bring to Your CX Defense

We work in environments where people and organizations are motivated to seize today's pennies forgoing tomorrow's dollars. This is a contributing factor as to why so few companies are customer-centric. Becoming customer-centric not only requires the Three Competencies – Identity, Intelligence and Consistency – but the patience to allow the competencies enough time to become culturally ingrained and to show results. In a "right now" world, becoming customer-centric is a long-term play.

So how does customer experience (CX) avoid becoming the next new thing that eventually fades into history? There are few factors in large organizations that win out over the temptation of seizing short-term gains to make the number and get a juicy bonus. Of course those in Accounting or Finance will always be able to quantify the upside of the short-term gain. What do you do when the organization is behind and looks like it is going to miss its revenue target and Finance comes to the table proposing going from 2-day to 5-day shipping, saving $19 million dollars this year?

Bring out the big guns

To fight this fight, you need big guns. Your big guns are Values, the correlation of the macro metric to a key financial metric, and Lifetime Customer Value. Values provide the soft defense while financial correlations provide the hard.

Values should be honored as if law. You can't go against your Values. This is a huge reason I push organizations to clearly define them. First, Values help in the delivery of consistent touchpoints and establishing the desired brand Identity. Second, Values are a parameter for decision-making. The very essence of Values is that they are foundational for all that the organization does.

Values represent a solid yet soft defense. Of course, Values can be a grey area where one can often argue both sides – this is why you also need hard metrics.

A hard metric

Lifetime Customer Value (LCV) is a hard metric. Understanding its components and drivers positions you to make a hard argument. Finance will be able to quantify the $19 million dollars savings to help "close the gap" or "make the number." You can use LCV or the one point movement in NPS calculation (see Resources Section) to quantify the other side of the story - the potential negative impact on customer value if the shipping proposal is accepted.

Without Values and/or financial correlations, what is your argument not to go to 5-day shipping and save $19 million dollars? Values and financial correlations will help an organization maintain its customer-centric compass when there are voices singing to seize the short-term financial benefits that will ultimately harm customers and their value to your organization.

> Note: There are a number of good articles and books on the subject
> of Lifetime Customer Value.

Competencies/Intelligence/Right Information/Macro Metric/Correlation

As part of the Intelligence Competency, it is critical to quantify your Customer Experience Management (CEM) efforts in financial terms. If you are in a large organization, it can be difficult to get the support of Finance executives for CEM without sound metrics that correlate to revenue.

81

Secret: The earlier you can tie CEM efforts to key financial metrics such as top-line revenue and show ROI, the sooner you will gain the depth of commitment needed to actually make significant changes, and if desired, transition to a customer-centric culture that establishes a competitive advantage.

Note: An original formula for correlating a one-point movement in Net Promoter score and top-line revenue is in the Resources Section. The Brigman CX Correlation Formula™ can also work to correlate some of the other macro metrics to revenue.

Truth: Financial metrics move based on a variety of factors. Revenue can go down while your macro metric is increasing, and vice versa. Whatever your financial metrics are doing, a macro customer experience metric heading in the right direction is helping.

Competencies/Intelligence/Right Information/Macro Metric/ Drivers
Know your customer's journey
Your macro relationship metric, Lifetime Customer Value (LCV) and financial correlation are key metrics on strategic levels. To impact these metrics, you typically have to improve the experiences and touchpoints at a tactical level – where customers encounter them along their journeys with your organization. Right Information in this case includes:

- Identifying which experiences and touchpoints along customer journeys are drivers of:
  - Macro metric
  - Lifetime Customer Value
  - Customer journey progression
  - Selection
  - Repurchase (if applicable)
  - Positive word-of-mouth/recommendation
  - Identity
- How to improve the touchpoint drivers to better meet customer needs

Build listening posts along customer journeys

A productive way of gathering this information is through listening posts. A listening post is any point along a customer journey where the organization collects customer and/or employee feedback. The listening post occurs at a touchpoint, and the survey itself is a touchpoint. Listening post surveys are typically short and very targeted in their focus. For instance, the survey at the end of a call to a call center is a listening post to gather feedback on the performance provided during that phone call.

Listening Post
Any point along a customer journey where the organization collects customer and/or employee feedback

Internal touchpoints and their infrastructure impact customer experiences and metrics

As the definition of touchpoints implies, touchpoints don't just happen between your organization and customers. Interactions – communication, physical, human and sensory – also happen *within* your organization.

There is an infrastructure to the development and deployment of touchpoints. This infrastructure includes the policies, processes, procedures and systems within which touchpoints are developed and delivered.

Improving touchpoint infrastructure typically enhances efficiencies, reducing expenses. Listening posts can often provide insights into infrastructure opportunities. A common misnomer regarding Customer Experience Management is that it is expensive to implement. While there certainly can be additional costs, successful CEM will also create efficiencies, saving resources.

> *There is nothing so useless as doing efficiently
> that which should not be done at all.*
> Peter Drucker

Truth: Through Customer Experience Management, the interconnectivity of the organization is revealed, along with its corresponding inefficiencies.

Deep Dive: Touchpoint Efficiency/Infrastructure Example – Saving $500,000

My team came across an interesting discovery when improving the experiences of new small business customers of a Fortune 30 telecommunication firm. We were examining how to improve the touchpoints of those small business customers that signed up for a bundle of services.

We found that for each of the services that made up the bundle, the customer received a welcome letter and other introductory communications via postal mail. With so many letters, customers started to view mailed communications from the phone company as junk mail. This conditioned customers to ignore communications. As a result of an infrastructure that didn't account for multiple, overlapping communications, customers occasionally ignored mail that actually contained important information.

Touchpoint Infrastructure
The policies, processes, procedures and systems within which employees, vendors and partners work to develop and deliver touchpoints.

Saving a half million on stamps

One of our recommendations was to combine these welcome and introductory messages into a single mailed piece. This provided a dramatically improved customer experience, a key goal, but it also resulted in a savings of over $500,000 a year *in postage alone.*

Over and over, using the implementation process detailed in *TOUCHPOiNT POWER*, I have led efforts that not only improved customer touchpoints and customer journey results, but saved the organization time, effort and/or money.

Truth: It is typically more cost effective to deliver better customer experiences and touchpoints.

Rule: A comprehensive Customer Experience Management Plan covers both customer and internal touchpoints as well as the organization's touchpoint infrastructure.

Secret: Measuring the resultant improvements of internal efficiencies can be an important means of measuring the success of CEM.

Include VOIC in your Intelligence

Listening posts along customer journeys capture VOC (voice of customer). At the conclusion of important customer experiences or journeys, it is also important to capture VOIC (voice of internal customer). At the conclusion of the complaint process, or after onboarding a new client, producing a conference, conducting training, launching a new product, or completing an annual promotion, survey all employees involved in the process.

Voice of internal customer (VOIC) efforts are important for gaining insights into reasons for both customer problems and internal inefficiencies.

VOIC typically examines both infrastructure – the policies, procedures and systems by which staff are required to operate – and the individual staff themselves. It is through VOIC that challenges in departmental cooperation – and their reasons – typically surface.

Just as it is important to have a macro customer relationship metric, it is also important to establish a VOIC macro metric that provides insight into the overall health of colleague teamwork and cooperation.

> Note: An example of a VOIC macro metric is detailed in the How To Section.

Mini Rant: VOC can (and sometimes needs to) Start Voice of Internal Customers

I was working with a new client that couldn't wait to get started on their gorilla Voice of Customer (VOC) metrics. In our assessment or discovery step, it was clear that everyone wasn't playing well in the company sandbox. Customer Service pointing fingers at Regulatory – they were taking forever to serve customer complaints. In fact, their internal processing of complaints was so bad that they were *getting complaints about their complaint process*. This, after two efforts to examine and improve their complaint process. Think about that. But I digress.

Sales was pointing fingers at Accounting – customers commenting that the people in Accounting weren't always pleasant. Customer Service and Sales pointing fingers at each other for not being responsive to each other and for not being customer-focused.

My recommendation was to start with VOIC – voice of internal customer (the employees). Start with 360 degree reviews of an experience such as

85

complaints. Have the review cover the processes, policies, and systems as well as individuals. Name names and get the dirt out on the table.

As it turned out, their problems were multifaceted. Part of the problem was individuals, and part internal systems and policies. It is amazing the change in behavior that can be created when individuals know that they are going to be evaluated on their customer service and teamwork. Again, "what gets measured gets done."

This organization was not ready for VOC. They might have uncovered amazing opportunities from their customers but their inability to work together internally would have inhibited their ability to fully capitalize on those opportunities.

Truth. Sometimes your best VOC program needs to start VOIC.

Relevance increases interest

The right information is relevant information. If an employee is receiving customer feedback that is not relevant to them, then human nature is to start to tune out the feedback. The relevance of available Intelligence is critical to all levels of decision-makers. Make sure information educates or is actionable. In other words, the information helps the employee understand something important about customers and their responsibilities, or, based on the information, they can take specific action. Additionally, it is important for those acting on touchpoint or experience intelligence to see and understand how the information and their prospective action ladders up to additional metrics and strategies.

Right Information to the Right People – the better database questions

Cost is typically a question and barrier around the topic of consolidating customer information currently residing in separate databases. It is expensive. Better questions around this topic include how a technology investment can help us:

- Advance our Values and/or Identity
- Improve customer engagement, service and touchpoints
- Upsell and grow Lifetime Customer Value

We work in an ROI world. Model these factors and couple them with your Values to make a solid business case for database consolidation.

Rant: The Annual Customer Satisfaction (CSAT) Survey

For those that do survey customers, the typical process historically has been the classic annual (or periodic) customer satisfaction (CSAT) survey. This antiquated process often measures mediocrity (satisfaction) while gaining information about issues that arose up to 12 months prior. The results take time to collect, months to analyze, and additional months to report out. Then, it is time to develop action plans around issues that, while probably still a problem, are old and dated. While this might include "right information," it is not the "right time." If your organization is just now learning about and taking action on problems that happened up to 18 months ago, it is not customer-centric.

> **Customer Feedback is a Gift**
> Janelle Barlow and Claus Moller wrote the book, *A Complaint Is a Gift, 2nd edition*, Berrett-Koehler, 2008. I couldn't agree more. Any customer feedback – especially a complaint – is a gift. And your first response should always be, "thank you."

This is a real-time world, and customer centric organizations understand their customers – their needs and their drivers – on a real-time basis. Customer-centricity involves listening to customers when and where they are positioned to quickly provide valuable feedback, and when, where and how they are willing to do so. And it involves making it easy and as painless as possible for the customer to provide you with the gift of their feedback. Their input is a gift that needs to be appreciated and valued as such.

The resultant action plans that come out of the "old school" periodic research programs are typically assigned to people that already are busy with their full-time jobs. What is their enthusiasm level likely to be for a new project to add to their already full plate?

Rule: Your first response to any customer feedback should always be, "thank you."

CSAT survey is often the opposite of customer-centric

If you can't tell, I am not a big fan of the typical annual or semi-annual survey. These are dinosaurs that deliver little value and create enormous amount of internal work, churn and consternation. Worst of all, this is not customer-centric. These surveys are typically long and arduous. And when asked questions, customers develop expectations. Nothing is worse than asking your customers what will help, having them take their valuable time and effort to provide you with relevant and actionable ideas, and then take a ridiculous amount of time to act on that valuable feedback.

From my experience, it is not uncommon for organizations to ask customers what they can do to improve, and then not take any action on the results. Then ask again, and again not take action. Then, ask again. Eventually customers stop telling them about their issues and the company can actually start to think that either the issue isn't important anymore, or that they have somehow miraculously addressed it. This, even though they haven't done anything about the problem at hand.

This is another example of a strategy-to-touchpoint gap. Colleagues in market research can do a great job of collecting data and turning it into strategic intelligence, but are typically powerless to see their intelligence turned into changes, especially at the touchpoint level.

Kill the dinosaur

Customers don't like these annual events and few employees are putting up their hands to volunteer to implement the action plans that arise. For the time, cost and churn, stop these events immediately and allocate these resources to a much more customer-centric research process. Establish a macro metric, correlate it to revenue, and uncover drivers at the touchpoint/experience level through ongoing listening posts and get this information to the right people in real time for immediate action.

Competencies/Intelligence/Right People

Right people

Everybody doesn't need all of the data collected – it can be overwhelming. While relevance involves the right information, it also involves the right people. Outside of macro goals and the macro relationship metric, people should work with information that is relevant specifically to them and their world. This means that they can *either act on the information, or it builds insight that can be applied to planning.*

To get the right information to the right people the information is typically parsed

Alerts

A system whereby a relevant employee is notified of a dissatisfied customer or negative customer touchpoint or experience that needs attention – sometimes referred to as "hot sheets."

in one of two ways. First, it can be parsed centrally. In other words, the person receiving the information is getting information that someone else determines is important. The alternative is that the information is aggregated into a single data base that is accessible by everyone. Here, departments or individuals can then slice and dice the information as they want or need. Users can typically develop standard templates, dashboards or reports. The ability to customize enhances the utility of the data, aiding right information to the right person.

Competencies/Intelligence/Right Time
Right time

Right time is typically the greatest challenge. Getting actionable data six months after the event is not customer-centric. Right time refers to both generating intelligence on a timely basis and responding in a timely manner through a closed-loop system.

Closed-Loop System
Input from customers systemically processed with results communicated back to the customer

When a dissatisfied customer or issue surfaces, the system should have the ability – through automation or manually - to get alerts to the right person in real time or near real time. Addressing the issue of an alert is not a chore, but an opportunity to solve a problem and create a happy customer, or to turn a dissatisfied customer into a satisfied one. It is also an opportunity to better understand what needs to be done to avoid the same problem in the future (addressing root cause).

Consolidate information into a dashboard

Just like other disciplines, departments or groups, customer experience will benefit from a dashboard of key metrics. Much more on this in the How To Section.

Rule: Develop a customer experience dashboard to help your organization better understand customer experiences, trends, and drivers along Relationship and Transactional Journeys. Where possible, tie these experience metrics to finance metrics.

Competencies/Intelligence/Summary

Building the Competency to generate and deliver the right information to the right people at the right time enables your organization to establish a closed-loop system to address time-sensitive individual customer issues. This Competency also helps to solve problems at the root cause, improving consistency. Listening posts covering both voice of customer (VOC) and voice of internal customer (VOIC) help in the planning and building of more customer-centric and efficient customer journeys.

Key points

To build a robust Intelligence system that will advance your customer-centricity and Lifetime Customer Value, couple a solid macro metric with the ability to correlate it to revenue and ongoing listening posts that:

- Uncovers the drivers of the macro metric
- Quantifies the performance of those drivers
- Surfaces and delivers alerts in real time for immediate action (closed-loop system)
- Surfaces infrastructure opportunities
- Feeds a CX dashboard

CHAPTER 5:
THE CONSISTENCY
COMPETENCY

Build a Touchpoint Structure
& Standardize Touchpoints

Consistency is the differentiator

Many organizations can and do perform admirably at defining and living their Identity. Some do a good job gathering and applying Intelligence. Only those who *consistently* deliver standardized touchpoints achieve true customer-centricity. This requires a Touchpoint Structure.

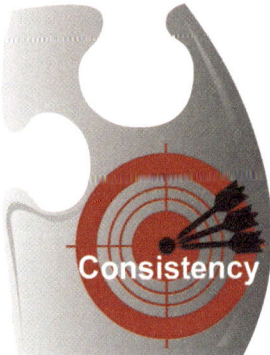

Truth: Consistency is the differentiator in achieving customer-centricity and is the source of a Touchpoint Structure.

Rule: Standards address inconsistency

Being consistently customer-centric can take many forms. Efforts to be consistent need to address the areas in which organizations typically perpetuate inconsistency. This means being:

- Consistent in understanding and meeting customer needs
- Consistent in the application of the defined Identity

91

- Consistent across all touchpoints along the entire holistic customer journey
- Consistent touchpoint performance regardless of which employee delivers the touchpoint

Mini Rant: Make Experiences Consistent with Marketing Communications

Marketing communication also needs to be consistent with customer touchpoints and/or experiences. Years ago the package delivery company DHL ran a prominent ad campaign claiming that they were "putting service back into the delivery business." One ad showed a DHL delivery driver taking his shoes off as he sought to quietly deliver a package to a library.

One day during the ad campaign I saw a DHL truck and went up to the driver. I asked what type of training he had gone through to help fulfill the ad campaign's promise. He laughed. There had been no training. It appears as though marketers decided to promote a new Identity without the organization building the ability to deliver on the promise – there was obviously no Touchpoint Structure to address this strategy-to-touchpoint gap.

Consistency across same or similar touchpoints

Consistency with touchpoints can take many shapes. We have already discussed two employees who approach returning customer calls in an inconsistent manner. For Hewlett-Packard, an audit of its products uncovered inconsistency in its navigation controls – enough different controls to fill a 4'x8' poster. The inconsistency in this physical touchpoint prompted development of a single standard control – the Q Control.

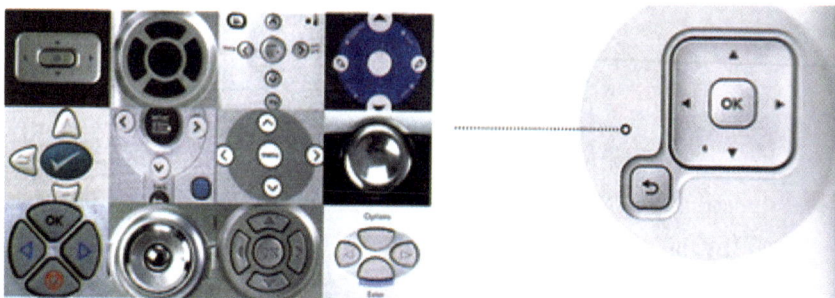

Image copyright (2012) Hewlett-Packard Development Company, LP. Reproduced with Permission.

Hank Brigman

Consistency in performance can include expecting the same taste and portion size of the same dish at a favorite restaurant or at different locations of the same restaurant.

If you think about the iconic customer-centric organizations – Apple, Disney, Nordstrom, Intuit, etc. – the greatest contributor to their iconic customer-centric status is their consistency. Across each touchpoint they are consistently customer-centric – you don't get a sense that you are fighting them to accomplish your goal. You also consistently get a strong sense of who they are – their Identity. Their touchpoints deliver value to both the customer and organization.

Competencies/Consistency/Touchpoint Principle
Introducing the Touchpoint Principle™

I capture and summarize what is needed to address the core problem and avoid the Inconsistency Problem Chain in what I call the Touchpoint Principle:

The ability to get and keep desired customers and employees is enhanced by consistently delivering Valued Touchpoints™.

Inconsistency Problem Chain™

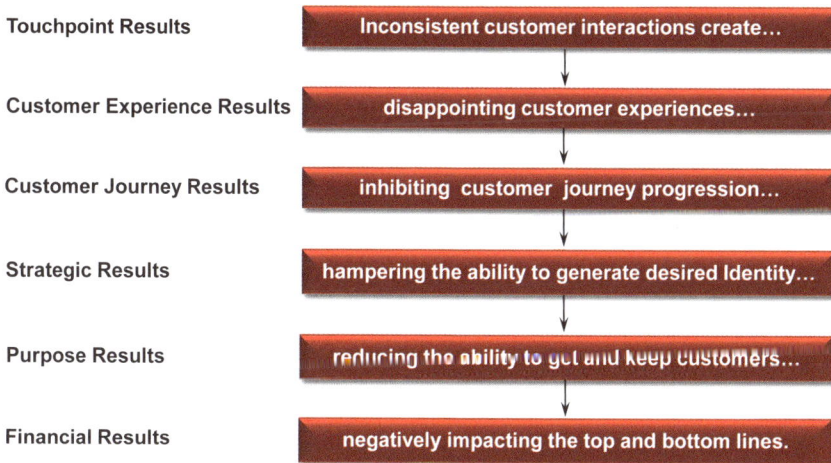

Touchpoint Results	Inconsistent customer interactions create…
Customer Experience Results	disappointing customer experiences…
Customer Journey Results	inhibiting customer journey progression…
Strategic Results	hampering the ability to generate desired Identity…
Purpose Results	reducing the ability to get and keep customers…
Financial Results	negatively impacting the top and bottom lines.

Competencies/Consistency/Touchpoint Principle/Valued Touchpoints

Valued Touchpoint: A standardized interaction that is customer-centric while advancing the organization's Values, Identity and Experience Strategy, and the touchpoint's goal(s).

93

Get away from whack a mole

Too often efforts to improve customer experiences are like an old boardwalk game, "Whack a Mole." A customer problem surfaces, and it is whacked/addressed, only to resurface again and again.

While several "moles" or customer experience problems can eventually be addressed, there is often organizational disappointment in the results. There can be a miss-directed expectation that desired customer behavior would improve once several problems are addressed.

Addressing a couple of prominent customer problems always helps, however, there are typically other problems that customers need to have "whacked."

Eliminating the problems that pop up will not drive the greatest behavior change. The greatest change comes in delivering the Touchpoint Principle™.

The ability to get and keep desired customers and employees is enhanced by consistently delivering Valued Touchpoints™.

The Touchpoint Principle™

The ability to get and keep desired customers and employees is enhanced by consistently delivering Valued Touchpoints™.

Valued Touchpoint

A standardized interaction that is customer-centric while advancing the organization's Values, Identity and Strategy, and the touchpoint's goal(s).

Think of your relationship with your significant other

For many businesses, *getting* a customer is like getting a date. It can take some work, and for some, more work than for others. *Keeping* a customer is like getting engaged. One good or great date, one gift, one trip together isn't typically going to get someone to commit to marriage. Likewise, one good touchpoint or experience typically isn't going to get a customer to make a commitment of loyalty.

For personal relationship engagement and customer relationship loyalty it takes the *consistent* delivery of Valued Touchpoints. Chances are whacking a few problems as they arise isn't going to change customer or personal behavior.

Deep Dive: The Touchpoint Principle and Valued Touchpoints

All about getting and keeping more customers

The Touchpoint Principle has four key components to examine.

1. First, the Principle focuses on advancing the purpose of business – getting and keeping customers – according to renowned management guru, Peter Drucker.

2. Secondly, it adds "employees" to Drucker's famous quote. Multiple case studies repeat the finding that improving customer-centricity enhances employee satisfaction and retention, and vice versa.

Mini Rant:
Are you on a Path to be left with an Organization of Samuels?

Remember Sarah, the employee who returns customer calls in two hours, and her colleague Samuel, who returns calls in two days? Which one do you think will leave the company first?

In my opinion, Sarah will leave first. She is inherently customer-centric. Some people have that attitude as a part of their makeup. The company she currently works for doesn't match her personal commitment to customer service. It probably galls her that she sits next to people who don't hold her same commitment to customer service.

Since Sarah's company won't promote or enforce customer service standards that are comfortable to her, she will go find a company that does. Interestingly, this scenario leaves this company with the type of employee who thinks calling a customer back in two days is a customer service best practice. Over time, the Sarah's of the company will continue to leave and the Samuels will continue to stay, and stay and stay. As customers, we engage with Samuels all of the time – employees that are just riding their job for a paycheck and can't wait until closing time.

Truth: The ability to attract and keep good employees is a key contributor to an organization's ability to get and keep customers, and vice versa.

3. Third, the Touchpoint Principle addresses the Core Problem. A third component of the Touchpoint Principle is consistency. In order to improve customer-centricity, the core customer experience problem of inconsistency must be addressed.

4. Fourth, the definition of a Valued Touchpoint has a defined hierarchy. The definition is: A standardized interaction that is customer-centric while advancing the organization's Values, Identity and Experience Strategy, and the touchpoint's goal(s). In priority order, the hierarchy is:

    1. Standardized
    2. Customer-centric
    3. Values
    4. Identity
    5. Experience Strategy
    6. Goal(s)

Valued Touchpoint hierarchy: 1. Standardized. To address the core problem of inconsistency, touchpoints must be standardized. Standards address inconsistency. More on this momentarily.

> **Truth**: The ability to get and keep good employees is a key contributor to an organization's ability to get and keep customers, and vice versa.

Valued Touchpoint hierarchy: 2. Customer-centricity. For a touchpoint to be valued by the customer, it must meet their needs. Customer-centric organizations' touchpoints are comfortable – customers don't have a sense of fighting the touchpoint to accomplish their goal. This is true regardless of the nature of or type of touchpoint, e.g. phone, web, human, etc. Customer-centric organizations gather and apply the Intelligence needed to know their customers and their customers' needs. As a result, they seem to anticipate needs at each touchpoint along customer journeys. In helping customers fulfill their needs, customer-centric organizations actually aid progression and conversions along customer journey stages.

How do we know where to put trash cans?

Through observation, Disney understands where their guests will typically need a trash can. They watch as guests purchase food and other items at outlets throughout their parks and where they then typically need a trash can. They have taken this intelligence and applied it to trash can location. The guideline is every 50' along pathways and every 25' along higher density entertainment venues, with guest use-patterns driving final placement. Rarely will a guest who has trash have to search long for a receptacle or go far out of their way to dispose of trash.

This example also highlights a typical ancillary benefit of good Customer Experience Management – greater efficiency. While this customer-centric approach to trash cans helps Disney's guests, it also cuts down on the amount of trash Disney employees have to pick up off the ground. This saves Disney time, effort and resources.

Listening doesn't always surface the best answer

To know your customers and what they need, you have to listen *and observe.* The first time I had to swipe my own credit card years ago at the grocery store rather than handing it to the clerk to swipe, I found it awkward. I wasn't use to doing it and it didn't come natural to me. Subsequently, I appreciated the time savings and the ability to retain control of my credit card.

If surveyed, I am sure that speed through check-out would have surfaced as one of my desires at most retail stores. Yet if asked, I certainly wouldn't have come up with the solution of conducting my own credit card transaction. However, by *observing* the check-out process, retailers were able to see the time wasting activities. Getting customers to handle the credit card transaction while the clerk rings up the items manages two activities simultaneously, saving time and improving the experience.

Valued Touchpoint hierarchy: 3. Values. Like the values you personally hold dear and live, organizations have and exhibit values. Customer-centric organizations have not only clearly defined their Values, but have integrated these into the fabric of their company. Their Values are a part of employee orientation, training, evaluation and promotion. They are talked about during meetings and, most importantly, exhibited by leaders.

Valued Touchpoint hierarchy: 4. Identity. Customer-centric organizations have a clear understanding of how they want to be perceived – the perceptual asset they want to create in the mind of the customer – and how they want customers to feel about them. These organizations are who they are across all of their touchpoints.

Identity and Values must be compatible. Each touchpoint should advance, or at a minimum, not conflict with or detract from either Identity (who you are) or Values (what you stand for).

McDonald's has a clear Identity

When you think of organizations with a consistent Identity, it is hard not to include McDonald's. Driving this Identity are the seven core Values Ray Kroc used to build the business:

- We place the customer experience at the core of all we do

97

- We are committed to our people
- We believe in the McDonald's System
- We operate our business ethically
- We give back to our communities
- We grow our business profitably
- We strive to continually improve

In their Standards of Business Conduct, they write, "Inherent in each value is our commitment to be ethical, truthful and dependable."

Is there any global business you know that is as "dependable" as McDonald's? Their consistency is legendary, and it helps to drive and define their Identity.

Valued Touchpoint hierarchy: 5. Experience Strategy. Organizations should have a long-term strategy in addition to their Operation and Experience Strategies. Valued Touchpoints serve to help, or at least not hinder, organizational efforts to achieve its long-term strategy while delivering on its Experience Strategy.

Valued Touchpoint hierarchy: 6. Goals. Along the Three Customer Journeys (Relationship, Transactional and Value Add), both your organization and your customer have goals to achieve. Customer-Centricity (second in the Valued Touchpoint hierarchy after standardize) addresses meeting customer goals. Your goals also have to be a consideration at touchpoints.

If the customer is on a Transactional Journey to potentially purchase or repurchase, you want the customer to complete that purchase (if it is in their best interest) and have it be a positive experience. Goals for an email may be that the recipient open and read the email and then click a link to access a specific web page. Once on the web page, the goal may be that the email recipient completes a form to download a white paper.

The goal of a thank you note can be just to make a good, warm impression that increases satisfaction or loyalty.

The goal of a sign on a display near the checkout of a retail store may be to prompt an impulse purchase.

As a touchpoint is designed, it is always important to keep its goal in mind.

A change in priorities

Notice that the goal of the touchpoint – i.e. have the customer click on a link – is last in the hierarchy of a Valued Touchpoint. This is opposite of how most touchpoints are developed and evaluated. Typically, the primary or only consideration in developing a touchpoint is the goal of the organization for the touchpoint – and don't think customers don't notice.

It's all about value

Valued Touchpoints in service of the Touchpoint Principle deliver value to both the customer and the organization. This is consistent with the definition and purpose of Customer Experience Management:

> The discipline used to comprehensively manage a customer's journeys with your organization, product, brand or service in the efficient creation of value for both customer and organization

Truth: The Consistency Competency is the means to transition an inconsistent touchpoint into a Valued Touchpoint.

More of exactly how to build a structure for developing and deploying Valued Touchpoints in the next section.

Competencies/Consistency/Touchpoint Principle/Valued Touchpoints/Value Chain

The Core Problem inhibits the purpose of business

A Customer Experience Management (CEM) Plan based on your Experience Strategy and delivering on the Touchpoint Principle will address the core experience problem – inconsistency – and the resultant Problem Chain

Inconsistency Problem Chain™

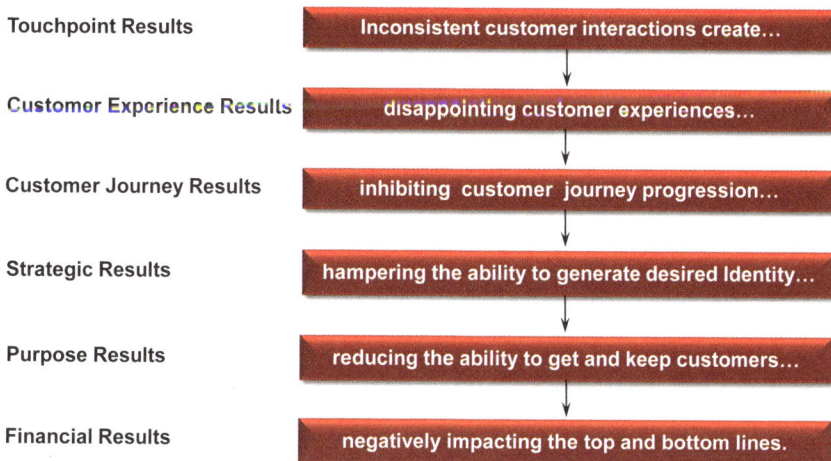

Touchpoint Results	Inconsistent customer interactions create...
Customer Experience Results	disappointing customer experiences...
Customer Journey Results	inhibiting customer journey progression...
Strategic Results	hampering the ability to generate desired Identity...
Purpose Results	reducing the ability to get and keep customers...
Financial Results	negatively impacting the top and bottom lines.

In addressing the Problem Chain, a Touchpoint Structure drives the Touchpoint Principle and creates a Value Chain:

Touchpoint Structure Value Chain™

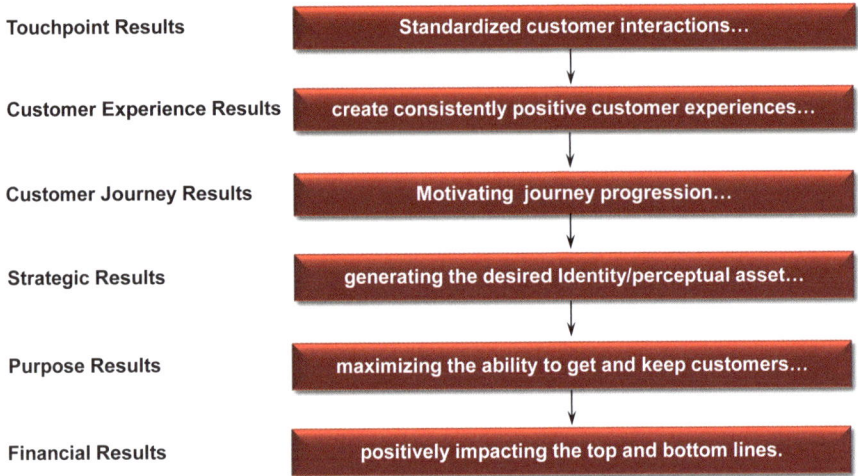

Touchpoint Results	Standardized customer interactions…
Customer Experience Results	create consistently positive customer experiences…
Customer Journey Results	Motivating journey progression…
Strategic Results	generating the desired Identity/perceptual asset…
Purpose Results	maximizing the ability to get and keep customers…
Financial Results	positively impacting the top and bottom lines.

The solution is standards

It is through a Touchpoint Structure of setting standards that your organization can deliver Valued Touchpoints. As the diagram shows, Valued Touchpoints enhance experiences, which accelerate progression of customers through their journeys. More customers advancing further in their journeys translates into getting and keeping more customers, and generating greater revenue and profit.

Some touchpoints are already standardized

Chances are standardizing touchpoints is not foreign to your business. When a customer calls one of your published phone numbers, how is the phone answered? Standardized? For most organizations, the answer is yes. How the phone is answered is standardized because we don't want employees answering however they want – we want to create the right impression. We don't leave individuals to decide how they answer the phone such that we might get, "Whacha want?"

Yet this is what is done with the bulk of touchpoints – the standard of performance is left to the individual. This is how a customer-facing employee can conclude that it is a best practice is to return a customer's call in two days (remember Samuel).

If we allowed individual employees to define performance across the product manufacturing journey, we would forever be creating products with different standards and characteristics. Yet, this is exactly what we do across customer journeys. We deliver inconsistent touchpoints that confuse our customers as to who we are – our Identity/perceptual asset.

Standardizing touchpoints doesn't mean that the standards are exact or the same for all customers. Standards can be a parameter – a sales clerk can discount an item between 5% - 15%. Standards can be individualized – does the patient want their appointment reminder via phone, email or text?

Competencies/Consistency/Summary

The Consistency Competency is the foundation of a Touchpoint Structure – the key to customer experience as a differentiator and competitive advantage. The importance of consistency is captured in the Touchpoint Principle: *The ability to get and keep desired customers and employees is enhanced by consistently delivering Valued Touchpoints.*

The Competency of building a Touchpoint Structure and delivering on the Touchpoint Principle achieves the resultant Value Chain that customer-centric organizations enjoy.

Key Points

- The Consistency Competency is the differentiator and the source of a Touchpoint Structure

- The Touchpoint Principle summarizes what is needed to address the core experience problem of inconsistency

- A purpose of the Consistency Competency is to transition inconsistent Touchpoints into Valued Touchpoints

- The hierarchy of Valued Touchpoints places customer needs above those of the organization

- A Touchpoint Structure creates a Value Chain

- Standards are the solution to the core experience problem of inconsistency

- Most organizations already standardize some touchpoints

SECTION III:

HOW TO ACHIEVE CUSTOMER-CENTRICITY

A Proven Implementation Model for

Getting & Keeping More Customers

SECTION III:

HOW TO ACHIEVE CUSTOMER-CENTRICITY

With an understanding of CEM foundations, the Three Customers-Centricity Competencies, Touchpoint Structure and Valued Touchpoints, it's time to dig into exactly how to develop and implement each.

To do so, we turn to a proven implementation model. This four-step model guides you through the process of assessing the current state, developing and implementing a Customer Experience Management Plan, and measuring results.

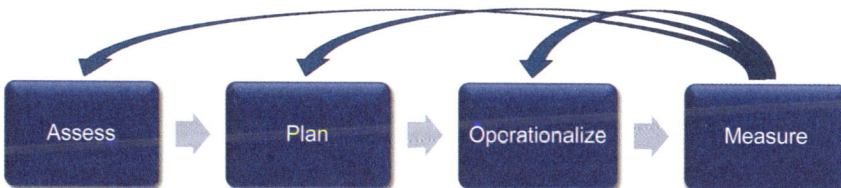

A focus of this section will be the four steps to develop a compelling Experience Strategy as part of the Plan step. The primary vehicle for the Operationalize step, Valued Touchpoint Workshops™ (VTW), is also detailed.

To help communicate the How To process, this Section follows a fictional company, Good Intentions Financial Technology (GIFT), as they launch their Customer Experience Management (CEM) journey for their B2B and B2C software business. The company and people are fictional. While the challenges faced and personalities encountered are drawn from my experiences, any resemblance to real companies or people is coincidental.

To make GIFT as relevant to as many readers as possible, GIFT distributes through retail, B2B field sales and reseller channels. GIFT also provides software related services.

Aspects of this How To Section will be stories of how the fictional characters in this fictional company approach the challenges and opportunities at hand. It is my goal that these people and stories provide context and a deeper understanding of why steps are taken.

This Section is broken into five chapters. The first chapter introduces GIFT and the Touchpoint Structure Implementation Model™. This is followed by chapters covering how GIFT applies each of the model's first three steps: Assess, Plan and Operationalize. The Operationalize Chapter includes a real life case study. The details of the fourth step, Measure, are incorporated into the chapters covering the other three steps.

Lastly, Chapter 10 explores how to get started – how to take that first or next step given your real world circumstances. While the story of GIFT is taken from real-world experiences, it is an almost perfect scenario. There is much we can learn from GIFT's journey, however, not all CEM opportunities start with such strong foundations. This last chapter provides insights on exactly where to start given your organization's circumstances.

After reading this How To Section, you will have a solid understanding of the model and its components and concepts. You will know exactly how to develop an Experience Strategy and build the Three Competencies, including a Touchpoint Structure. You will also have insight into where to start – your first step. In other words, you will know *how to* become customer-centric.

As with all aspects of *TOUCHPOiNT POWER*, you will need to customize the concepts, ideas and tools presented in this section to meet the needs of your unique situation.

The Power of Touchpoints

Poorly implemented changes cost Netflix 74% of its value

Netflix was a company that got it. They were innovative in their approach to providing movie videos to U.S. customers' mailboxes.

Customers loved the simplicity of their online ordering model. There were no hidden fees and issues were quickly addressed. Customers were loyal and promoted the service – they loved Netflix as a result of both their Operation and Experience Strategies. Netflix Operation and Experience Strategies built a "Blue Ocean" differentiation and competitive advantage on model innovation and low cost such that they basically put brick and mortar video stores out of business.

But customer loyalty is not blind. Netflix's 60% price increase for those customers with both DVD and streaming subscriptions was problematic, but applying it without explanation was a horrible implementation step. The late apology was coupled with a new bombshell – the company was splitting its streaming and DVD businesses into two separate entities. Yet the two businesses couldn't communicate with each other – customers were required to have separate log-in and password information for each. Netflix was now essentially two different organizations, each charging for their video service.

> **Blue Ocean Strategy** Generally refers to the creation by a company of a new, uncontested market space that makes competitors irrelevant and that creates new consumer value often while decreasing costs. It was introduced by W. Chan Kim and Renée Mauborgne in their best-selling book, *Blue Ocean Strategy: How to Create Uncontested Market Space and Make the Competition Irrelevant*. Boston: Harvard Business School Press.
>
> Source: http://lexicon.ft.com/ Term?term=blue-ocean-strategy

In implementing this new two-organization structure Netflix lost sight of its customer-centricity. The company that had built its loyalty on being simple, easy and customer friendly appeared to have been taken over by aliens.

The results

By the time Netflix eventually abandoned its two business model, significant damage was done. Netflix went from an all-time high of $304.69 per share in July (SF Chronicle) around the time of the price increase, to $77 on October 25 (Wall Street Journal). This drop of over $200 per share represents a loss of market cap of about 74%. Ouch!

107

Netflix was an example of a company that demonstrated that they knew "how to" achieve customer-centricity. However, once achieved, customer-centricity must be maintained and nurtured. Unfortunately, their focus became rather self-centric rather than customer-centric. At the time, they abandoned their Values and Identity and implemented policies and delivered touchpoints that angered their customers, who responded by defecting.

Truth: While customer-centricity is hard to achieve, it is easily destroyed by abandoning the foundations of Values and Identity.

Key assets to overcoming crisis

Both Netflix and Toyota are examples of how a strong and positive Identity can help an organization overcome crisis. For Toyota, it was horrible results and press over its accelerator problem and corporate cover-up of the problem. Yet both Netflix and Toyota survived, and eventually thrived again. For both, customers came to their defense because of the strong Identity and resultant relationship with the brand.

Truth: Strong and positive Identity and relationships will be invaluable assets in the face of an organizational crisis.

CHAPTER 6:
A PROVEN
IMPLEMENTATION MODEL

A Company at a Crossroad and Their Choice of How To
Differentiate & Build a Defendable Competitive Advantage

Model/GIFT
Good Intentions Financial Technology (GIFT) –
A company with challenges

Good Intentions Financial Technology (GIFT) serves its United States
and international customers, clients and resellers from its headquarters
in the Western U.S. In GIFT's most recent year end, it recorded annual
revenue of $560,000,000 on 0.3% growth. About half of GIFT's rev-
enue is generated in the U.S. market.

Serving both consumer and business customers

Products/Services. GIFT sells and services accounting software. It sells:

- GIFT Home & Small Biz, an out of the box solution to track fam-
  ily, sole proprietor and small business finances

- GIFT Enterprise, a cloud-based solution for medium and large
  businesses

GIFT trains and supports its Enterprise clients via its maintenance and
service programs and products.

109

Multiple customers via retail, direct and resellers

Distribution. GIFT offers its Small Biz accounting software online and as a retail product through office supply stores. Office supply stores are served by GIFT's Strategic Accounts, a small group within its sales department that also serves select accounting firms that resell its software to their clients. GIFT has its own field sales staff selling to GIFT Enterprise clients. Customer Service and Technical Support provide call center, staff training and legacy or other systems integration for its Enterprise product.

Cloud Based Computing
Internet-based computing in which large groups of remote servers are networked so as to allow sharing of data-processing tasks, centralized data storage, and online access to computer services or resources.

Source: Dictionary.com

Slowing growth in a stagnating market

Situation. GIFT is a middle of the pack player in each of its markets. For years GIFT rode the rapid growth rate of the accounting software market. GIFT's position as a lower-cost option served it well. While it grew dramatically during those golden years, its growth rate and market share trailed its primary competitors. In recent years, the accounting software market growth rate has softened dramatically. GIFT's sales and profits have stagnated and to this day continue to trail competitors.

GIFT faces stiff competition from organizations focused exclusively on one of its markets (e.g. small business) and much larger organizations competing directly with GIFT across each of its markets. Originally an enterprise-only provider, GIFT recently added the technology for its Small Biz product through acquisition.

Model/GIFT/SWOT
Strengths – fast follower with tenured employees and customers

GIFT has a legion of tenured and dedicated employees. Several Enterprise clients who have been with the company for years serve as references. A fast-follower, GIFT has recently transitioned their Enterprise product from server to cloud-based following several of its major competitors.

Weaknesses – lack of a differentiator

Rapid expansion during the growth years coupled with the addition of several new board members and a recent acquisition have created natural challenges. During the expansion the firm built a new building anticipating continued growth. One third of the space stands empty and the resultant debt is a growing financial burden. As the market's growth rate flattened, GIFT's competitors lowered prices, forcing GIFT to lower its prices further to remain the lower-cost competitive option. This eroded profits. There have been a number of unflattering posts on social media sites regarding GIFT's products and service as it works out bugs in the transition of its Enterprise product to the cloud. GIFT's use of low price as its differentiator has surfaced as a strategic problem and is a focus of several new board members.

Opportunities – small business and maintenance

GIFT's entry into the small business segment positions it to meet customer needs across the entire market. There now also exist the opportunity to grow its new small business customers into its Enterprise product.

GIFT's maintenance program is a high profit margin service, yet renewal rates are lower than industry benchmarks. This is especially true of Tier 3 service-level customers. GIFT offers three levels of maintenance/support. Tier 3 is the lowest level of support offered and the attrition rate of these customers is significant. Tier 3 offers no direct support, only software updates and an online message board and FAQs (frequently asked questions).

Threats – low cost pressures

GIFT's threats were not insignificant.

1. Continued positioning us a lower-cost economic choice in a mature market with strong and well-funded competition.

2. Lack of a clear differentiator as an option to price on which to market, sell and grow.

3. Shrinking profits limiting ability to address significant debt from the recent acquisition and new office building.

111

Model/GIFT/Early Steps
The story of GIFT's survival

This story of GIFT's use of CEM to build customer-centricity as a competitive advantage starts with the recognition that it needed to better differentiate.

The decision and first steps

President Maggie Rawle came out of the board meeting with a furrowed brow, but with a clear charge – differentiate or die.

She sat down at her desk, made room for her ever present Diet Coke, and started to examine the three options for differentiation:

- Price
- Quality/Innovation
- Service/Experience

Price was already a losing proposition. Larger and better-funded competition could lower prices for a period of time and potentially bury GIFT.

Having just completed the Enterprise product's transition to the cloud and integrated the small business acquisition into the organization, GIFT didn't have the additional capital to increase investments in research and development (R&D) in order to differentiate on quality/innovation. The accounting software category was relatively mature and customers were no longer clamoring for specific and significant improvements. Larger competitors would probably be able to quickly match any technological improvement they made, eliminating any long-term benefit.

Maggie chooses service

With price and quality/innovation not attractive differentiators, Maggie chose to differentiate across customer service/experience. A smile came to her face as she decided that she would build a truly customer-centric organization.

Maggie read books, visited two iconic customer-centric organizations and launched a search to find someone to head efforts to transition GIFT to become more customer-centric.

Not finding the executive level customer experience talent externally, Maggie promoted Paul Hem to lead efforts. Paul had been Director of Project Management prior to being tapped to coordinate the integration of the small business acquisition into GIFT. Paul was very well

respected and knew how to get things done at GIFT. His new title – Vice President Customer Experience.

Building critical ingredients

With a customer experience leader in place, GIFT's had a committed chief executive and internal political expertise. Maggie knew she needed to add Customer Experience Management (CEM) expertise and resources.

In launching the new CEM group, Maggie budgeted for two staff and an operational budget of $500,000 that included money for hiring a CEM coach for Paul.

Originally Maggie planned for the new group to report up through the marketing organization. After her research, she decided instead to position the group independent of any department, with Paul reporting directly to her.

Through her research, Maggie picked up some key points to pass on to her new VP Customer Experience.

Keep your allies close...

Maggie knew that their CEM efforts would have both allies and enemies and that it is best to turn to allies for early wins and/or to conduct pilots. She had learned that the greatest Customer Experience Management (CEM) allies often lie in those departments along customer journeys that are viewed as expense departments. Call centers and distribution can be receptive CEM allies. They are forever being pressured to cut their costs and are accustomed to examining processes.

While "sales" is typically the primary beneficiary of CEM efforts, they are usually bandwidth-constrained. They are under pressure to introduce new products or messaging, and always under pressure to make their numbers. As a result, sales can be hesitant early on to embrace their needed contribution to CEM efforts. The "expense-only" departments typically welcome help improving their customer service and internal efficiencies (although they may feel they have done it all already).

In her meeting with Paul, Maggie shared these insights and summarized this lesson: Know who is on your side and help them generate wins.

...and your frenemies closer

Maggie also cautioned Paul to know who does not embrace his CEM efforts.

Secret: Just as with customers, don't start with trying to convert internal detractors into promoters.

Truth: That said, nothing will help credibility more than turning an internal detractor into a promoter.

In closing their first one-on-one, Maggie tasked Paul with providing the Executive Council (EC) with an overview of CEM that would get the organization's leaders on the same page. She would set up an EC meeting with CEM as the only agenda item.

Model/GIFT/EC Presentation
Getting leaders on the same page

Paul had presented to the Executive Council (EC) a number of times, especially on his work managing the integration of the acquired home and small business accounting technology into GIFT's system. However, this was different. Paul was now expected to present on an area in which he had little or no expertise. He was grateful that Maggie budgeted for a CEM coach and membership in an association of customer experience professionals. Between books, his CEM coach and the association he came up with a presentation for the Executive Council (EC) to lay out the problem and opportunity.

> Note: Visit *www.TouchpointPower.com/Resources* for a list of customer service/experience associations.

The presentation would cover the basics:

- Problem
- Desired state
- Solution
- Nomenclature
- Process
- Benefits

Start with the problem

Paul knew that the EC was well aware of their lack of a differentiator problem and the decision to focus on customer service/experience as the differentiator. He quickly touched on this as background prior to launching into the problem.

Paul started by sharing that the core customer experience problem is inconsistency and that most organizations, including GIFT, do several things that actually perpetuates inconsistency. He then described a desired state for GIFT: A state where they were truly customer-centric, a state where their customers and employees loved them and spoke glowingly of the company, and a state where they were growing rapidly, receiving industry accolades and large bonuses.

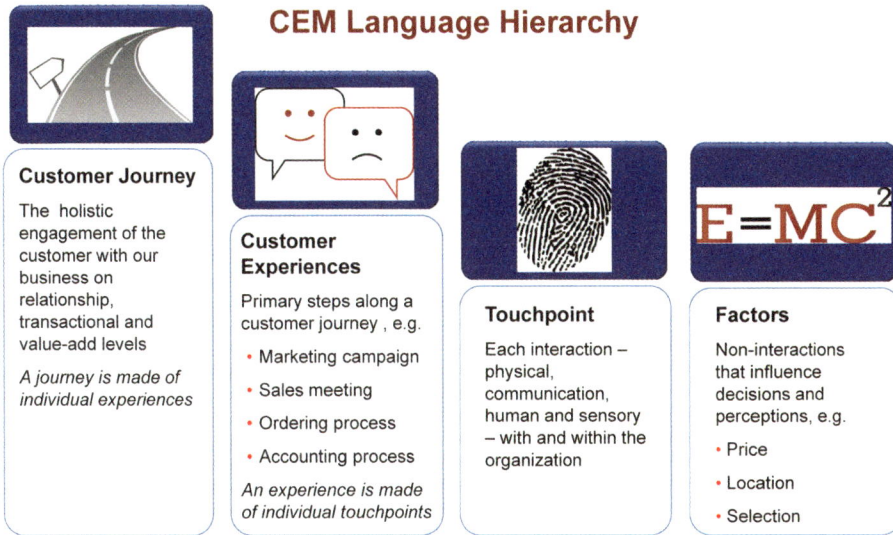

CEM Language Hierarchy

Customer Journey

The holistic engagement of the customer with our business on relationship, transactional and value-add levels

A journey is made of individual experiences

Customer Experiences

Primary steps along a customer journey , e.g.

- Marketing campaign
- Sales meeting
- Ordering process
- Accounting process

An experience is made of individual touchpoints

Touchpoint

Each interaction – physical, communication, human and sensory – with and within the organization

$$E = MC^2$$

Factors

Non-interactions that influence decisions and perceptions, e.g.

- Price
- Location
- Selection

Paul introduced CEM as a new discipline, the solution to the problem and the means for achieving the desired state. He defined the CEM language hierarchy and explained that he was recruiting the EC to use and help support and enforce the correct use of the terms.

Paul presented the Touchpoint Principle and the importance of Valued Touchpoints. He explained that in this new Touchpoint Economy GIFT must understand the holistic customer journey and deliver customer-centric touchpoints that are valued, and that promote journey stage progression.

Then, Paul laid out the process for tackling this opportunity:

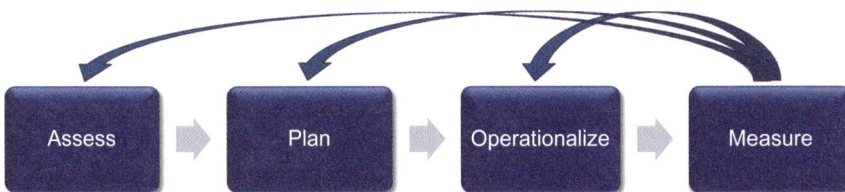

Assess → Plan → Operationalize → Measure

Paul explained that he would be engaging an outside firm to conduct an independent assessment and that the assessment would form the basis for their CEM Plan.

Impressive list of benefits

The benefits to achieving the desired state through successful CEM were significant: Ability to differentiate, decreased cost of customer acquisition, reduced churn, greater revenue

---
Customer Experience Management Plan

The plan to achieve the Experience Strategy through building the Three Customer-Centricity Competencies™, including a Touchpoint Structure.

---

per customer, improved employee satisfaction and retention, greater efficiencies, and a better bottom line.

Following a robust question and answer period, members of the EC expressed their appreciation for the presentation and support for his approach. Maggie reiterated the importance of CEM to the organization and the need for support from this group for Paul's efforts.

Note: A generic version of Paul's introductory deck is available for free download: Doc # 060, CEM Introduction Deck, *www.touchpointpower.com/resources*.

Deep Dive: The Touchpoint Structure Implementation Model

The Touchpoint Structure Implementation Model is designed to enable delivery of the Touchpoint Principle, solve the core problem and realize the benefits of the resultant Value Chain.

Touchpoint Principle: *The ability to get and keep desired customers and employees is enhanced by consistently delivering Valued Touchpoints.*

The four steps of the Touchpoint Principle Implementation Model are standard steps for most process models – the titles may be different, but the gist of these types of models is somewhat generic. What is important is what is done within this model to maximize the probability of Customer Experience Management (CEM) success.

This four-step model covers:

- Assessing the current state
- Developing a compelling Experience Strategy and comprehensive Customer Experience Management (CEM) Plan

- Implementing a CEM Plan that achieves the Experience Strategy and builds the Three Competencies, including a Touchpoint Structure

- Measuring success

The major components of the steps of the Model are:

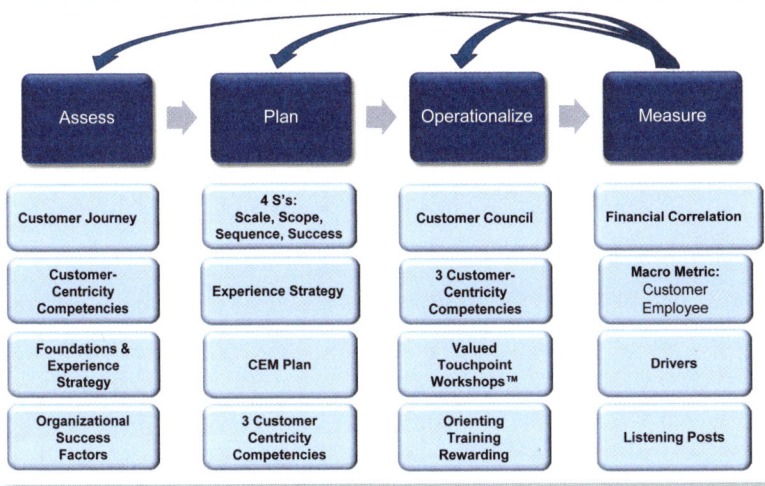

Assess	Plan	Operationalize	Measure
Customer Journey	4 S's: Scale, Scope, Sequence, Success	Customer Council	Financial Correlation
Customer-Centricity Competencies	Experience Strategy	3 Customer-Centricity Competencies	Macro Metric: Customer Employee
Foundations & Experience Strategy	CEM Plan	Valued Touchpoint Workshops™	Drivers
Organizational Success Factors	3 Customer Centricity Competencies	Orienting Training Rewarding	Listening Posts

Paul was ready to get started.

Model/Summary
Key points

- There are four steps to the Touchpoint Structure Implementation Model:

    - **Assess.** Assessing the current state.

    - **Plan.** Developing a compelling Experience Strategy and comprehensive Customer Experience Management (CEM) Plan.

    - **Operationalize:** Implementing a CEM Plan that achieves the Experience Strategy and builds the Three Competencies, including a Touchpoint Structure.

    - **Measure:** Measuring success.

- Keep your allies close and your frenemies closer

- An initial executive presentation to align leaders can cover the basics:

  - **Problem.** The core experience problem and how organizations perpetuate the problem.

  - **Desired state.** What the situation would be like if the problem where solved.

  - **Solution.** How to solve the problem.

  - **Nomenclature:** Introduction of the language of Customer Experience Management (CEM).

  - **Process.** The solution's process or model.

  - **Benefits.** Specific benefits to the organization and individuals.

CHAPTER 7
MODEL STEP 1,
ASSESS

Auditing the Current State

Assess

Assess/Audit
Audit to Assess four areas

Paul's first step in the Touchpoint Structure Implementation Model (TSIM) is to Assess or audit where GIFT stands – its current state. In this step, he and his selected vendor will conduct a Customer-Centricity Audit. The Audit will focus on assessing four areas:

1. **Customer journey.** Assess how GIFT is performing along the Customer Relationship Journey.

2. **Competencies.** Assess the status of each of the Three Customer-Centricity Competencies – Identity, Intelligence and Consistency.

3. **Strategy.** Assess whether the organization has defined each of the four components of an Experience Strategy – Purpose, Objective, Position and Live.

4. **Organization.** Assess needs across five organizational success factors – Independence, Support, Resources, Expertise and Political Acumen.

> **Customer-Centricity Audit:**
>
> Assessing the customer-centricity of an entity across its performance along the seven stages of the Customer Relationship Journey; the status of the Three Customer-Centricity Competencies; existence of each of the three components of an Experience Strategy; and status of each of the five organizational success factors.

The vendor explained that their sources of information would include:

- Internal systems and sources
- Employees
- Customers
- Channel partners
- Vendors
- The marketplace (analysts, etc.)
- Owners

A solid foundation for planning

A key purpose of the Assess step is to establish a foundation for developing both the Experience Strategy and Customer Experience Management (CEM) Plan. Both will be developed during the Plan step based on a thorough knowledge of the current state gleaned during the Assess step.

Assess/Audit/1. Customer Journey
Assessing with an eye to identifying potential pilot projects

Paul planned to examine the efficacy of the entire current Customer Journey, looking to identify two areas.

1. Customer problems:
   a. Where in the journey do customers complain most?
   b. Where in the journey do employees feel that customers have the greatest problems?

2. Immediate financial opportunities:
   a. Where in the journey are there experiences that can have the greatest short-term financial impact if inconsistent touchpoints are transitioned into Valued Touchpoints?

This aspect of the Assess step is designed primarily to surface projects to pilot that will address *customer* opportunities while also have the potential to deliver a significant ROI. Both Paul and Maggie knew that early ROI success was critical to combat colleagues skeptical of CEM efforts – those who view CEM budgets as better applied to their own or other projects.

Low-Hanging fruit identified

As expected, the vendor's Customer Journey Audit turned up low-hanging fruit that could be targeted for early wins. Audit results were communicated to Paul in a report that included simple color-coded dashboards for recognition and presentation purposes.

> Green = Yes, excelling or accomplished
>
> Yellow = Partial or in progress or unknown
>
> Red = No, deficient or non-existent
>
> Note: Items that don't clearly qualify for one of the three colors will be depicted by two colors – either green and yellow or Red and yellow.

Pilot Program

An experimental program designed to test administrative and operational procedures and to collect information on service demands and costs that will serve as a basis for operating programs efficiently.

Source: www.answers.com

Truth: One of the most important decisions impacting the strength and duration of CEM efforts will be which project(s) to tackle first (pilot).

For GIFT's Getting and Keeping stages of the Customer Relationship Journey, the vendor identified the following as most deficient:

Customer-Centricity Audit: Customer Journey	No	Partial/In Progress	Yes
Getting			
Home & Small Biz			
In-store shopping experience	☐		
Online e-commerce	☐		
Enterprise			
Enterprise sales process – sales force effectivenes	☐		
Compelling case studies	☐		

121

Customer-Centricity Audit: Customer Journey	No	Partial/In Progress	Yes
Keeping			
Home & Small Biz			
Post registration of a Small Biz product	■		
Prep for office supply retailer's annual planning process	■		
Enterprise			
Onboarding new Enterprise customers	■		
Onboarding new accounting firm reseller partner	■		
Maintenance – Tier 3	■		
User training	■		
Software updates	■		

Paul knew that as GIFT builds its Intelligence competency, it will learn much more about how it is performing along the holistic customer journey. The primary purpose at this point is to identify where to focus initial projects.

Assess/Audit/2. Competencies

Building the Three Customer-Centricity Competencies (Identity, Intelligence and Consistency) is a key focus of the Customer Experience Management Plan. As such, it is important to understand the starting point or current state across each of the Competencies.

Paul's vendor conducted its Audit of the Three Competencies across 38 factors.

Assess/Audit/2. Competencies/Identity

In Assessing the first of the Three Competencies, Identity, the vendor worked to determine where GIFT stood on each of the four structural Foundations of the Identity Pyramid: Values, Identity, Vision and Mission.

While Paul was disappointed in the results, the vendor let him know that the results were quite typical. For GIFT, several of the foundations had been codified, but much work remained.

Identity Pyramid™

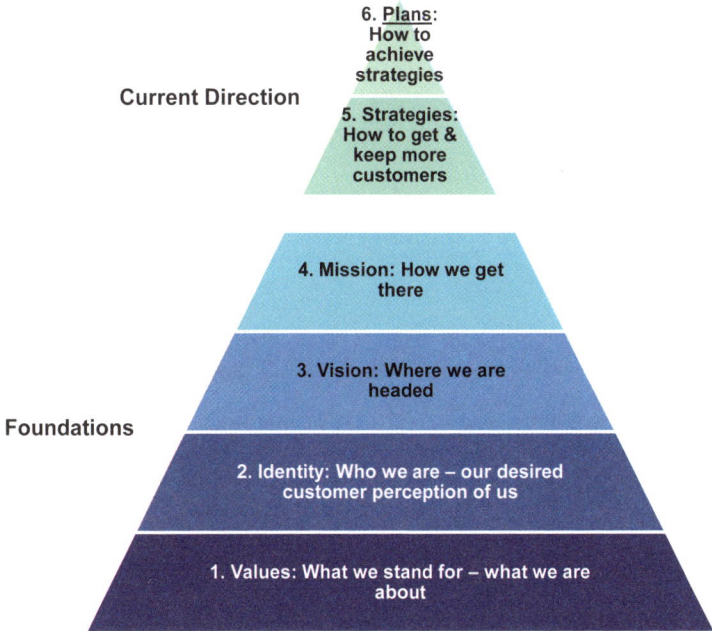

6. Plans: How to achieve strategies

5. Strategies: How to get & keep more customers

Current Direction

4. Mission: How we get there

3. Vision: Where we are headed

Foundations

2. Identity: Who we are – our desired customer perception of us

1. Values: What we stand for – what we are about

Identity - Define & Live	No	Partial/ In Process	Yes
Values have been defined - what we stand for	No		
Identity has been defined - who we are	No		
Vision has been defined - where we are headed			Yes
Mission has been defined - how we get there (Vision)			Yes
Strategies defined - how to get & keep more customers		Partial	Yes
Plans developed - how to achieve strategies		Partial	Yes
Examples of staff living Values/Identity are celebrated	No		
Values/Identity applied to planning/ decision-making	No		
Values/Identity communicated internally	No		
Values/Identity applied to hiring/orienting	No		
Values/Identity applied to evaluating/promoting	No		
Values/Identity applied to rewarding/compensating	No		
Values/Identity applied to training	No		
"Customer Council" meets regularly	No		

123

Assess/Audit/2. Competencies/Intelligence

In Assessing the current state of the Intelligence competency, the vendor Audited the scope, timeliness and relevance of information gathered, as well as its application.

Intelligence - Right Info to Right People at Right time	No	Partial/ In Process	Yes
Macro customer metric defined and implemented		yellow	green
Macro customer metric correlated to financial metric	red		
Macro customer metric known by all	red		
Macro customer metric prominent at executive meetings		yellow	
Macro employee metric defined and implemented	red		
Feedback generated on individual employee teamwork	red		
Listening posts collect VOC & data at key touchpoints	red	yellow	
Market/Competitive intelligence infrastructure established		yellow	green
Timely macro metric & listening post feedback generated	red	yellow	
Timely staff feedback generated	red		
Relevant/actionable macro metric feedback generated		yellow	green
Relevant/actionable listening post feedback generated	red	yellow	
Relevant/actionable staff feedback generated	red		
Closed-loop system for customer & staff feedback to drive immediate action	red		
Voice of customer applied to planning	red	yellow	
Staff data & feedback applied to planning		yellow	
Customer Experience Dashboard established	red		

Assess/Audit/2. Competencies/Consistency

In this aspect of the Audit, the vendor examined how well GIFT standardizes touchpoints – in other words, its Touchpoint Structure.

Consistency - Standardize Touchpoints	No	Partial/ In Process	Yes
Touchpoints are consistently mapped and evaluated	■		
Touchpoints standardized	■		
Touchpoint best practices codified	■		
Touchpoint standards & best practices incorporated into employee orientation & training	■		
Touchpoints customer-centric		■	
Touchpoints advance Values & Identity	■		
Touchpoints advance Experience Strategy	■		

As a result of the Audit, Paul could see that there was a lot of work to do. He knew that a purpose of his Customer Experience Management Plan would be to prioritize where to focus initial efforts across each of these Audit criteria. His Plan needed to turn each factor green.

Assess/Audit/3. Experience Strategy

The vendor examined the existence and relevance of each of the four elements of a compelling Experience Strategy:

1. **Purpose** (why). Why the organization is undertaking CEM – which organizational goal does CEM efforts support/drive?

2. **Objective (what).** What is CEM to accomplish?

3. **Position (where).**

   A. Where is the current state Experience Position?

   B. How does it align with the Brand/Offering Position and the positions of key competitors?

   C. Where is the desired state Experience Position?

4. **Live (how).** How to design and deliver touchpoints (guidelines often called "service standards")?

The results of the audit of GIFT's Experience Strategy were in line with where Paul thought they would land.

Experience Strategy	No	Partial/In Process	Yes
Purpose - why CEM			
Objective - what is CEM to accomplish			
Position - where experiences are positioned in the marketplace			
Live - how organization develops and delivers touchpoints (i.e. service standards)			

There was already some clarity as to purpose and objective, but defining GIFT's Experience Position and how it would "live" its strategy had yet to be codified.

Assess/Audit/4. Organization

For this part of the Assessment, the vendor examined where GIFT stood across five success factors: independence, support, resources, expertise and political acumen.

Rant: Customer Experience Management (CEM) and Your Organization – the Five Organizational Success Factors

So many organizations start out with the best of intentions when it comes to their Customer Experience Management (CEM) efforts. Many trip over unforeseen organizational challenges.

Maximizing CEM success involves five organizational success factors:

- Independence
- Support
- Resources
- Expertise
- Political acumen

Independence – a standalone department

First, CEM shouldn't be in a department. Customer journeys traverse departments and CEM needs to have line of sight to the entire journey and deal on equal footing with all of the departments along customer journeys. If CEM resides within one of the departments, it hinders success and collaboration. CEM should reside as a stand-alone function.

Support – organization leader must lead

IBM in-depth interviews with hundreds of business executives around the world found:

- "Top-down, ongoing support of senior executives and clear links to overall corporate goals" was one of the most critical factors that differentiated successful initiatives

- Nearly three out of four companies designate ownership of CEM initiatives with sales, marketing, IT or some other department

- Only a quarter of firms assign it to a corporate-level team

- If CEM is owned at the corporate level it has a 25 percent to 50 percent greater chance of success

Source: Q&A with Don Peppers and Martha Rogers: Measuring Customer Value Can Be More Important than Measuring Revenue (3/2/2006) CRM Project Volume 6, by Don Pepper, Martha Rogers, Peppers & Rogers Group

Independence and support is best represented by a direct reporting relationship to the chief executive who not only talks the talk, but walks the walk.

Resources – budget helps positioning

Positioning is important. Your CEM group, department or team should be positioned as there to help others succeed. There will be problems if the team is viewed as adding work or requiring or expecting significant efforts from others. The team needs to focus on how it can help those working along the customer journey improve their customer touchpoints and infrastructure, making their work life better.

To aid its position as a helper, the CEM team needs resources with which to work. The team will be embraced if it can bring people and/or budget to contribute to facilitating improvements.

Expertise and Acumen – knowing what and how

lastly, CEM success needs both CEM expertise and political acumen. CEM expertise is knowing *what* to do to succeed. Political acumen is knowing *how* best to get it done in the organization.

There are three options to combine expertise and acumen:

1. CEM expertise in-house with strong political mentors and advisors

2. Tenured in-house personnel in CEM positions with external CEM expertise engaged on an ongoing basis as a coach and/or consultant/vendor

127

3.Mix of CEM expertise and tenured professionals on the in-house team plus some external expertise hired as/if needed

Each of the three options can work. The key is that you have large and ongoing doses of both CEM expertise and internal political acumen.

Rule: To maximize success, set CEM efforts up independent of other departments and provide solid leadership support, resources, expertise and acumen.

GIFT's organizational results were outstanding. The vendor found that the department was independent, enjoyed executive leadership support and resources, had a CEM coach for needed expertise, and a leader who knew how to get things done within the organization.

Customer-Centricity Audit: Organization	No	Partial/ In Process	Yes
Indepence			
Support			
Resources			
CEM Expertise			
Political Acumen			

Assess/Summary
Key points

- A thorough Assessment of the current state helps define:
  - ☐ The low-hanging fruit along the Customer Relationship Journey
  - ☐ The needs for building each of the Three Competencies
    - ▽ Identity
    - ▽ Intelligence
    - ▽ Consistency
  - ☐ The existence of each of the four components of an Experience Strategy
    - ▽ Purpose (why)
    - ▽ Objective (what)

▽ Position (where)

▽ Live (how)

☐ The Status of each of the five organizational success factors

   ▽ **Independence.** A standalone group or department.

   ▽ **Support.** Chief executive that walks the talk.

   ▽ **Resources.** Budget and heads.

   ▽ **Expertise.** CEM.

   ▽ **Political acumen.** How to get things done in the organization.

Chapter 8:
Model Step 2,
Plan

Developing a Compelling Experience Strategy
and Customer Experience Management Plan

Plan

Plan/Introduction
Paul was going to take three steps:

1. Alignment. Get answers to four questions critical to strategy and
   plan development.

2. Strategy. Build a compelling Experience Strategy across each of
   the four components: Purpose, Objective, Position, and Live.

3. Plan. Develop a comprehensive Customer Experience Management (CEM) Plan to achieve the Experience Strategy.

Plan/Alignment
Get leaders to answer four critical questions

There are four critical questions covering: Scale, Scope, Sequence and
Success – the Four Ss. Paul knew that getting leadership to answer these
questions would further ensure alignment and serve the development of
GIFT's Experience Strategy.

Four Ss:

1. **Scope.** Department vs. organization.

   ■ Is the desire to improve the customer experiences of a specific department or responsibility, or the entire organization?

2. **Scale.** Experience vs. culture.

   ■ Is the desire to tactically improve some specific customer experience deficiencies, or to make a strategic move to shift to a more customer-centric culture?

3. **Sequence.** Speed vs. fact.

   ■ Is the desire to quickly address problems while building knowledge, or to gain the knowledge/facts before making changes?

   ☐ **Fact-based:** *Sequential* and diligent application of each of the four steps of the Touchpoint Structure Implementation Model. In this implementation sequence, the foundations of the Identity Pyramid and macro metrics and relevant listening posts are established *prior* to undertaking the primary "Operationalize" vehicle, Valued Touchpoint Workshops. With the Identity and Intelligence available, Valued Touchpoints can then be designed and delivered based on facts. The resultant Valued Touchpoints are truly customer-centric while advancing the organization's Identity.

   ☐ **Speed-based:** There is so much low-hanging fruit that there is little need to wait. Valued Touchpoint Workshops (VTW) are launched prior to Identity development, or gaining needed Intelligence, or both. Desired state touchpoints and process improvements will be based on available employee and customer input and Intelligence. Identity and Intelligence efforts will be undertaken concurrently with VTW's with results incorporated into the workshops when available. As a result, there may be a need to go back and recalibrate some Valued Touchpoints once the Identity and/or relevant Intelligence is available.

Valued Touchpoint Workshop (VTW)

A team of relevant colleagues mapping and evaluating the current state of touchpoints of an experience or journey (if a current state exists), and designing, implementing, promoting and measuring a desired state of Valued Touchpoints.

---

4. **Success.** Hard vs. soft.

- Is the desire to measure success with hard or soft metrics? In other words, will a soft macro metric (i.e. Net Promoter score) be the barometer of success, or will success be based on the CEM Plan's impact on a hard metric such as revenue?

Deep Dive: Speed or Fact-Based

The answers to the Four S questions are important in developing the Experience Strategy and CEM Plan, and to aligning the organization to CEM efforts. The results of *not* answering these questions were clear to me when I was contracted by a large financial services company.

Speed and Fact in conflict

This company had established a CEM team with the charge to make the organization more customer-centric. In the team's Assessment it became clear that there was an enormous amount of low-hanging fruit that could be addressed and that would positively impact customer experiences.

As a result, the CEM team had attempted to implement speed-based – tackling low-hanging fruit as quickly as possible. Yet as they attempted to move their CEM initiatives forward, they faced an enormous amount of internal resistance. This financial services organization was at its culture, fact-based. It was full of actuaries and analysts who demanded to know the factual basis for this team's proposed efforts.

Without getting executive leadership to answer the Four Ss, the CEM team ended up bucking the natural culture of the organization. They really didn't have a defense when asked why they wanted to move ahead without conducting thorough research with a high degree of confidence. It was obvious to them what needed to be done, but obvious didn't fly in this organization. Had they been given executive charge to implement speed based, they would have been in a position to constructively deal with the internal resistance they encountered.

Fact or speed-based decision needs to be made early as the choice dramatically impacts the CEM Plan and design of the initial CEM team/organization (the CEM team will be covered later in this section). Keys to the fact/speed decision include:

- The value and quality (or lack of quality) of current customer experiences

133

- The upside to CEM improvements – immediate improvements can benefit customers and provide a positive return on investment (ROI)

- Culture – a culture strongly geared toward finance and numbers may be better off implementing fact-based

- Market factors – a competitor that has made recent and dramatic customer service improvements that places your organization in a competitive disadvantage may dictate a speed-based implementation

Truth: Fact-based implementations require enormous patience on behalf of executives.

Executive engagement and answers to four critical implementation questions

Paul got on the agenda of an EC meeting and asked the Four S questions: Scope, Scale, Sequence and Success. After robust discussion, the Executive Council aligned on:

- Scope – organization (start in the U.S. and then roll out to international markets)

- Scale – culture

- Sequence – speed

- Success – hard (revenue)

Paul's next step – developing an Experience Strategy.

Plan/Experience Strategy

The four steps to developing an Experience Strategy

Paul knew that his CEM Plan needed a guiding strategy. His thinking follows the hierarchy of the top section of the Identity Pyramid. The top of the Pyramid, Current Direction, demonstrates that "Plans" serve "Strategies."

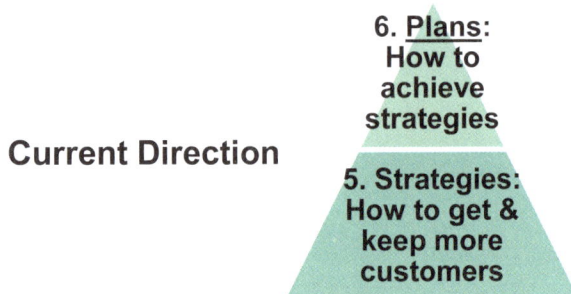

Current Direction

6. Plans:
How to
achieve
strategies

5. Strategies:
How to get &
keep more
customers

Hank Brigman

To help ensure buy-in and relevance, Paul recruited a small cross-functional team of colleagues engaged with customers to develop the Experience Strategy. The group included the VP of Marketing, a sales rep, a trainer and a customer service supervisor.

Plan/Experience Strategy/Template
A template to guide Experience Strategy development

Paul used a template based on answering the *why, what, where* and *how*:

To help drive our _____ (*why* – the purpose tied to a macro organizational strategy/objective) our Experience Strategy is to _____ (*what* it is to quantifiably accomplish) through positioning our service policies as _____ and our touchpoint execution as _____ (*where* we are positioned) and consistently delivering our _____ (*how* we live our Identity and Experience Strategy across customer touchpoints).

Plan/Experience Strategy/Template/Purpose
Purpose: Why?

Paul and the rest of the group knew that the Experience Strategy had to align with one of Maggie's overarching goals/objectives. As President, she has specific and tangible goals the organization is targeting and she emphasizes them every time she speaks to the organization. One of her objectives is to achieve 5% year over year growth.

The group felt that the Experience Strategy purpose is: *To help drive 5% year over year growth.*

> **Experience Strategy**
> *Why* we undertake CEM and *what* we seek to achieve through *where* we position both our service policies and the execution of customer touchpoints and *how* customers experience our Identity.

Plan/Experience Strategy/Template/Objective
Objective: What?

The next question to answer: Our Experience Strategy objective is to

_____.

Secret: Be careful of tying the objective to short-term goals. CEM is typically a long-term play and it is typically best to tie CEM to more strategic and long-term goals.

The EC's answers to the Scope and Scale Four S questions would help the team with objective parameters.

Scope – the EC choose organization over department
Scale – the EC choose culture over experience

Maggie was pushing her leaders to develop SMART goals and the team wanted to incorporate SMART goals into their Experience Strategy objective. The objective the team landed on:

To help drive 5% year over year growth, our Experience Strategy objective is to build a customer-centric culture such that within three years GIFT achieves and maintains the highest Net Promoter score (NPS) in each of our direct markets.

SMART Goals

SMART goals are Specific, Measurable, Attainable, Relevant and Time-bound.

Source: Wikipedia

Secret: Try to make the objective quantifiable. While this is not always possible, it is best to be able to measure the progress of achieving the Experience Strategy.

Plan/Experience Strategy/Position
Position: Where?

With the objective defined, the Experience Strategy team moved on to defining and aligning GIFT's Experience Position.

To help drive 5% year over year growth, our Experience Strategy objective is to build a customer-centric culture such that within three years GIFT achieves and maintains the highest NPS in each of our direct markets through **positioning our service policies as** _____ and our **touchpoint execution as** _____

To fill in these blanks, the team will need to answer:

- What is the current state Experience Position?
- How does it align with our Brand/Offering Position and the positions of key competitors?
- What is our desired state Experience Position?

To answer these questions, the team dove into the three exercises for defining an Experience Position:

1. Complete the Brand/Offering Position Map (see next page)

2. Complete the Experience Position Maps

3. Compare the Maps and define the desired state Experience Position

Brand/Offering
The organization's primary brand, product or service offering

Note: The term "brand/offering" covers the primary product or service.

Plan/Experience Strategy/Position/Brand.Offering Position Map

As a starting point, the team answered the two questions for the Brand/Offering Map.

Question 1. Quality: Compared to competitors, the quality of our primary brand/offering is…

- **Inferior.** The quality of one or more key aspects, features or functions of our primary offering is inferior to that of our competitors.

- **Equivalent.** Our quality is about the same as that of our competitors.

- **Equivalent Plus.** Our quality is about the same as that of our competitors with one key aspect, feature or function that is superior (and is typically promoted).

- **Superior.** In many or most cases, the quality of our offering's aspects, features or functions are superior to those of our competitors.

Question 2. Price: The pricing of our primary offering is...

- **Reactive.** We are without a pricing strategy and our pricing is primarily responsive to the pricing in the marketplace(s) in which we compete.

- **Discount.** We price lower than our competitors in an effort to compete and/or to achieve volume sales.

- **Competitive.** Our pricing is similar to that of our competitors.

- **Premium.** Our prices are higher than our competitors', reflecting the additional value we provide.

The team wrote "Current State" in the quadrant where the answers to Question 1 and Question 2 intersected.

Brand/Offering Position Map™				
Quality Position: Compared with our competitors, the quality of our primary offering is...	**Pricing Position: The pricing of our primary offering is...**			
	Reactive Responds to market	**Discount** Lower than competitors	**Competitive** Similar to competitors	**Premium** Higher than competitors
Inferior Slightly lower quality				
Equivalent Same quality		**Current State**		
Equivalent Plus Slightly better quality				
Superior Equal or better across all or most quality measures				

Plan/Experience Strategy/Position/Experience Position Map
Answer the next two questions to map your Experience Position

Next, the team answered the two questions for the Experience Position Map.

Question 3. Position: Compared to our competitors, our service policies (rules governing payments, qualifying for credit, returns, fees, complaints, etc.) are...

- **Inferior.** One significant service policy or many of our service policies are less customer-centric than those of our competitors.

- **Equivalent.** Our service policies are about the same as those policies of our competitors.

- **Equivalent Plus.** The bulk of our service policies are about the same as those of our competitors with one policy that is superior and typically promoted (i.e. Enterprise Rent-a-Car, "we'll pick you up").

- **Superior.** Several, many or most of our customer service polices are superior to our competitors.

Question 4. Execution references how well and consistently we tactically deploy touchpoints across our customers' journeys. In other words, how well we interact with customers and meet their needs at every level and across every department. Our touchpoint execution is:

- **Reactive.** There is no clear performance or execution expectation. Just like the Whack-a-Mole boardwalk game where the player attempts to hit moles that pop their heads up out of different holes, our organization hops reactively on the "hot" customer service or experience issue of the day. The quality of touchpoints is left to individual employees, which often lowers the level of performance to the least common denominator among staff.

- **Selective.** Our organization focuses on delivering a few specific touchpoints really well. As a result, there are some good, some bad, some really good, and some potentially really bad customer touchpoints. Customers don't know what to expect and are confused as to "who" our company is and what it is all about. Through feedback we hear that our touchpoints are inconsistent.

- **Siloed.** Our company has a department or group who "own" the customer relationship (often sales or service). The customer experience focus is on this group and their customer touchpoints. The "owners" do a good job with their touchpoints. However, when customers interact with other functions or departments, such as returns, accounting or distribution, it is often like dealing with another company. Because of an organizational focus on the "owners" of the relationship, touchpoints with the other departments are typically not as pleasant or successful as those interactions with the "owners." In addition to inconsistent customer experiences, siloed execution creates internal churn and friction between groups or departments.

> **Valued Touchpoints**
> Standardized interactions that are customer-centric while advancing the organization's Values, Identity, and strategy as well at that touchpoint's goals

- **Valued.** Our company realizes that it is the entire company that owns customer journeys and the resultant customer relationship. As owners of the relationship, each department and individual consistently delivers Valued Touchpoints.

These questions prompted much discussion among Experience Strategy team members. Both the sales and customer service reps provided the team with insights based on what they continually face or hear from customers. In answering the questions, the team wrote current state where the answers to Questions 3 and 4 intersect:

Experience Position Map™				
Policy Position: Compared with our competitors, our service policies are...	**Touchpoint Execution Position: Our execution is...**			
	Reactive Hit the pain	**Selective** Some great, some horrible	**Siloed** Good but different dept to dept	**Valued** Consistent across TPTs
Inferior One, some or many are less customer-centric	Current State			
Equivalent Same across all policies				
Equivalent Plus 1 Policy is better & promoted				
Superior Equal/better across all policies				

Note: it is not uncommon that the answer is between options, rather than fitting perfectly in a quadrant.

Deep Dive: Experience Position and Your Company

Your touchpoint execution (Question 4) impacts every customer. While the answers to each of the four questions are interrelated in their impact on success, your answer to Question 4 can provide important insights into the status or existence of your Touchpoint Structure. Of the four areas covered by the questions, Execution is typically where organizations need to focus action plans to better align the two maps/positions.

Note: Check below to further evaluate your organization's Execution Position (Question 4). Which description best describes your organization?

Experience Position Map™			
Touchpoint Execution Position: Our execution is...			
Reactive Hit the pain	**Selection** Some great, some horrible	**Siloed** Diff. experience dept to dept	**Value** Consistency across TPTs
Ours is a languishing company with poor morale and high customer and employee turnover.	Our is a confused company with confused customers.	Ours is an inconsistent and churning departmentalized company where each silo delivers their own level of service and there is a lot of internal finger pointing.	Ours is a company that enjoys a long-term and sustainable competitive advantage and as a result, is very successful.

Deep Dive: Position Alignment Critical to Success

To be properly aligned, the Experience Position must be the same or "better" – one quadrant below and/or to the right of the Brand/Offering Position (see the light grey in the map on the next page).

If your Experience Position is above or to the left of your Brand/Offering Position – like GIFT's on the next map – then the two are out of alignment (see white quadrants). You confuse your customers if the position of your service policies or touchpoint execution is worse than your primary offering.

An Experience Position two quadrants below or to the right of the Brand/Offering Position can be a marketable differentiator (see mid grey on the next map). Positions in the Valued column of the Experience Map differentiate and provide a long-term competitive advantage (see dark grey).

Eroding the investment in your product/service

An Experience Position that is out of alignment degrades or erodes the perception and position of the product/service/brand/offering. Organizations typically make significant investments in producing a product or codifying a service.

It doesn't make business sense to degrade the typical massive investment in product/service design, development and production by delivering service policies or touchpoints that are not in keeping with the offering's positioning.

141

Plan/Experience Strategy/Position/Map Comparison
Compare your two maps

The Experience Strategy team developed the following map to show the Experience Position alignment possibilities based on their Brand/Offering Position.

Experience Position Map™				
Policy Position: Compared with our competitors, our service policies are...	**Touchpoint Execution Position: Our execution is...**			
	Reactive Hit the pain	**Selective** Some great, some horrible	**Siloed** Good but different dept to dept	**Valued** Consistent across TPTs
Inferior One, some or many are less customer-centric	*GIFT*			
Equivalent Same across all policies	*Unaligned*	**Brand/Offering position**	*Aligned*	**Differentiator & long-term competitive advantage**
Equivalent Plus 1 Policy is better & promoted				
Superior Equal/better across all policies		**Potential**	**differentiator**	

A key tool in defining Experience Position

The comparison of the two maps provided insights. GIFT's Experience Position was not aligned with its Brand/Offering Position. It was a bit sobering for the team given the time, effort and money GIFT sinks into designing and developing its software products.

Where are competitors?

The team knew that GIFT's desired state Experience Position should not be developed in a vacuum. The next step involved overlaying competitors' positions on the two maps.

Comp = Competitor.

Brand/Offering Position Map™

Quality Position: Compared with our competitors, the quality of our primary offering is…	Pricing Position: The pricing of our primary offering is…			
	Reactive Responds to market	**Discount** Lower than competitors	**Competitive** Similar to competitors	**Premium** Higher than competitors
Inferior Slightly lower quality				
Equivalent Same quality		**GIFT**	Comp 1 Comp 2	Comp 4
Equivalent Plus Slightly better quality			Comp 3	
Superior Equal or better across all or most quality measures				

Experience Position Map™

Policy Position: Compared with our competitors, our service policies are…	Touchpoint Execution Position: Our execution is…			
	Reactive Hit the pain	**Selective** Some great, some horrible	**Siloed** Good but different dept to dept	**Valued** Consistent across TPTs
Inferior One, some or many are less customer-centric	~~GIFT~~			
Equivalent Same across all policies		Comp 2	Comp 1 Comp 4	
Equivalent Plus 1 Policy is better & promoted		Comp 3		
Superior Equal/better across all policies				

Most competitors are experienced challenged

The team was somewhat surprised to see that the majority of their enterprise competitors were also experience challenged. In fact, only Competitor 1 aligned its Experience Position with its Brand/Offering Position. This made some sense to the team as Competitor 1 was the strongest in the market.

In examining the competitive landscape, the team now had a better handle on how to position their experiences as a differentiator to create a defendable competitive advantage.

Deep Dive: Experience Position as a Competitive Advantage

Differentiating and reaping the benefits of a competitive advantage is possible when executing a "Valued" Experience Position (see the shaded Valued column below).

Experience Position Map™				
Policy Position: Compared with our competitors, our service policies are...	**Touchpoint Execution Position: Our execution is...**			
	Reactive Hit the pain	**Selective** Some great, some horrible	**Siloed** Good but different dept to dept	**Valued** Consistent across TPTs
Inferior One, some or many are less customer-centric				
Equivalent Same across all policies		Differentiator & defendable competitive advantage		
Equivalent Plus 1 Policy is better & promoted				
Superior Equal/better across all policies				

Overcome a misconception to generate a competitive advantage

It is a common misconception that a "Superior" Brand/Offering is required in order to deliver a Valued execution. In other words, many believe that a company must be premium-priced like The Ritz-Carlton or Rolls-Royce Motor Cars to benefit from delivering Valued customer experiences. While iconic service brands are typically positioned as Superior and Valued, the truth is that any organization can execute and benefit from a Valued Experience Position, almost no matter its Brand/Offering Position.

McDonald's defies convention

Think of McDonald's. Their service policy position is only "Equivalent," however, they excel at consistently executing Valued Touchpoints. Their bathrooms are consistently clean, staff well dressed and courteous, and they are obsessed with efficiency for both customers and the business.

How many other fast food providers have evolved the efficiency of the drive-through customer experience to the point where you may find two order lanes, separate payment and pick-up windows, and an automated machine dispensing beverages? When exiting the highway in the U.S. with the sole purpose to find a bathroom, which fast-food restaurant do you seek?

If we examine McDonald's Position Maps, we find that their Experience Position is better - one coordinate to the right – than their Brand Offering Position (see map below). As a result, their positions are aligned. Since their positions are aligned and include Valued execution, they enjoy a competitive advantage and are in a position to maximize their ability to get and keep customers.

McDonald's Position Maps

Brand/Offering Position Map™				
Quality Position: Compared with our competitors, their quality of our primary offering is…	**Pricing Position: The pricing of our primary offering is…**			
	Reactive Responds to market	**Discount** Lower than competitors	**Competitive** Similar to competitors	**Premium** Higher than competitors
Inferior Slightly lower quality				
Equivalent Same quality			McDonald's	
Equivalent Plus Slightly better quality				
Superior Equal or better across all or most quality measures				

Experience Strategy Map™				
Positioning Strategy: Compared with our competitors, our service policies are…	**Touchpoint Execution Strategy: Our execution is…**			
	Reactive Hit the pain	**Selection** Some great, some horrible	**Siloed** Diff. experience dept to dept	**Value** Consistency across TPTs
Unknown No position				
Equivalent Same across all policies				McDonald's
Equivalent Plus 1 Policy is better & promoted				
Superior Equal or better across all policies				

In a world of low-cost fast food options, McDonald's differentiates and enjoys a competitive advantage through their execution of Valued Touchpoints.

Plan/Experience Strategy/Position/Desired State
Defining the desired state Experience Position

With their Maps complete, the team was ready to determine its desired state Experience Position. The team didn't believe the benefits were there for a "Superior" service policies position and that it would be overly burdensome to achieve a "Superior" level of service policies in the short term.

145

The team felt that "Equivalent Plus" would deliver better value in the short term if GIFT could find the appropriate "plus" policy with which to differentiate.

The team was unanimous in its desire to transition to a Valued Execution. They mapped their Desired State.

Experience Position Map™				
Policy Position: Compared with our competitors, our service policies are...	**Touchpoint Execution Position: Our execution is...**			
	Reactive Hit the pain	**Selective** Some great, some horrible	**Siloed** Good but different dept to dept	**Valued** Consistent across TPTs
Inferior One, some or many are less customer-centric				
Equivalent Same across all policies				
Equivalent Plus 1 Policy is better & promoted				**Desired State**
Superior Equal/better across all policies				

(Current State → Desired State)

The team would present the EC with a proposed desired state Experience Position of Equivalent Plus and Valued.

Rant: Align the Policies of Your Experience Position to what is Practiced

It is not uncommon that as your Experience Position is defined, there may be numerous policies that are not consistent with the Position. If your Experience Position is to provide premium service to better align with your premium product positioning, then your service policies need to be at least at par, and for the most part, exceed those of your competitors. If your shipping policy trails that of your competitors, then the policy needs to change to align with your premium pricing and Experience Position. Otherwise, you are confusing your customers.

These types of changes can be challenging and can be perceived as expensive. However, how expensive is it to confuse your customers?

I worked with a client that had published hard and fast policies regarding the return of their products from resellers. Their return policy was more stringent and less customer-centric than their competitors despite the fact that they offered the higher priced premium product.

The actual policy is what is done, not what is written

Many of this organization's reseller customers also dealt with all of its competitors and were accustomed to the competitors' more relaxed return policies. When confronted with a refusal to accept products for return based on policy, this premium provider's reseller "customers" complained.

Interestingly, an analysis found that these complaints went through a number of levels of the organization internally before returns were actually granted almost 100% of the time.

The policy the company actually practiced was that if you complained enough, you could return their products. How would that make you feel as a customer? Customers eventually got what they wanted but were ticked off in the process for having to go through the hoops to get what they believed they deserved in the first place.

By actions do you guarantee satisfaction?

The same can be said of a satisfaction guarantee. Chances are if a customer isn't satisfied, you are going to return all or part of their money. If that is or would be your practice, why not promote the fact that you offer a satisfaction guarantee. I offer this type of guarantee and to date have never had a refund request. Yet this guarantee does provide prospects with peace of mind.

Truth: The internal churn and calisthenics we can put our customers through to eventually say yes is expensive on so many levels. Why not save the internal cost and negative customer experience and just align the policy with what is actually already done and promote the customer-centric policy?

Improving these types of policies requires planning that address timing, budget, implementation, training and internal and market promotion. Your Customer Experience Management Plan must consider these logistics to best accommodate prospective changes in customer service policies.

The team's working Experience Strategy thus far:

To help drive 5% year over year growth, our Experience Strategy objective is to build a customer-centric culture such that within three years GIFT achieves and maintains the highest NPS in each of our direct markets through positioning our service policies as equivalent plus and our touchpoint execution as Valued.

147

Plan/Experience Strategy/Live

Live: How?

With their Position exercises complete, the team moved on to completing the template by defining how they are to "live" their Experience Strategy.

To help drive 5% year over year growth, our Experience Strategy objective is to build a customer-centric culture such that within three years GIFT achieves and maintains the highest NPS in each of our direct markets through positioning our service policies as equivalent plus and our touchpoint execution as Valued **and consistently delivering our _____ (***how*** we live our strategy across customer touchpoints).**

The next step was to determine how to get their Strategy to "live" across each touchpoint on a much more granular and customer-focused basis. In other words, to capture the *characteristics of how the Strategy will live at each touchpoint.*

The team pulled an example from the hotel industry to gain a better idea of their targeted output.

The Ritz-Carlton Service Values

I am proud to be Ritz-Carlton

1. I build strong relationships and create Ritz-Carlton guests for life.

2. I am always responsive to the expressed and unexpressed wishes and needs of our guests.

3. I am empowered to create unique, memorable and personal experiences for our guests.

4. I understand my role in achieving the Key Success Factors, embracing Community Footprints and creating The Ritz-Carlton Mystique.

5. I continuously seek opportunities to innovate and improve The Ritz-Carlton experience.

6. I own and immediately resolve guest problems.

7. I create a work environment of teamwork and lateral service so that the needs of our guests and each other are met.

8. I have the opportunity to continuously learn and grow.

9. I am involved in the planning of the work that affects me.

10. I am proud of my professional appearance, language, and behavior.

11. I protect the privacy and security of our guests, my fellow employees and the company's confidential information and assets.

12. I am responsible for uncompromising levels of cleanliness and creating a safe and accident-free environment.

The team liked the internalization of Ritz-Carlton's Service Standards – the fact that each started with "I." They decided to call what they developed their "Touchpoint Promises."

Touchpoint Promises

I am GIFT and these are my Touchpoint Promises

1. *I recognize that I have customers to serve well both internally and externally*

2. *I live the "Golden Rule" as a foundation for positive and long-lasting customer relationships*

3. *I will be in my customer's moment, striving to understand them and their immediate and future needs*

4. *I own and will address my customer's problems and opportunities*

5. *I am consistently responsive, cooperative, courteous and accurate*

6. *I work and advise based on the customer's best interest*

7. *I adhere to our touchpoint standards and am empowered to develop and share best practices to improve customer experiences and internal efficiencies*

8. *I continuously learn and teach*

9. *I live and enforce our Code of Conduct*

10. *I am proud to represent GIFT and I will let that pride show in all that I do*

The team was pleased with the Experience Strategy they would propose to the EC:

To help drive 5% year over year growth, our Experience Strategy objective is to build a customer-centric culture such that within three years

149

GIFT achieves and maintains the highest NPS in each of our direct markets through positioning our service policies as equivalent plus and our touchpoint execution as Valued and consistently delivering on our Touchpoint Promises.

Deep Dive: Boiling it Down

The full Strategy can be a mouth full. While the detailed description helps to guide decisions and actions, it is important to boil the Strategy down to a simple statement or concept that is more memorable. Wells Fargo has a great example of this. Here is a picture of a sign posted in one of their banks.

It may be difficult to boil an Experience Strategy down to a single word – if possible, great – but it needs to be shortened to a phrase or sentence that is memorable, relevant and that serves the Experience Strategy.

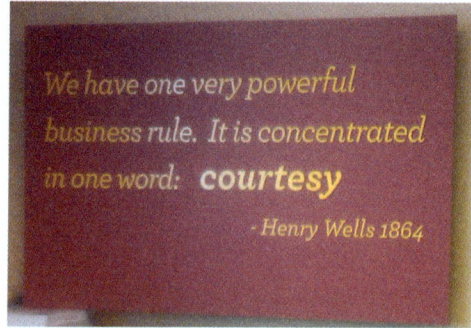

We have one very powerful business rule. It is concentrated in one word: **courtesy**

- Henry Wells 1864

Aligning the Experience Strategy

What can and should a boiled down version of the Experience Strategy represent? Your Identity. This aligns the Strategy with "living" the Identity.

Secret: Boiled down, an Experience Strategy represents the organization's Identity.

Deep Dive: Helping Employees at Every Level Know the Destination and How to get There

A well-articulated Experience Strategy serves to help both customers and employees. While the Strategy is applicable to every employee, its different components can be viewed as primarily serving/guiding different levels of the organization.

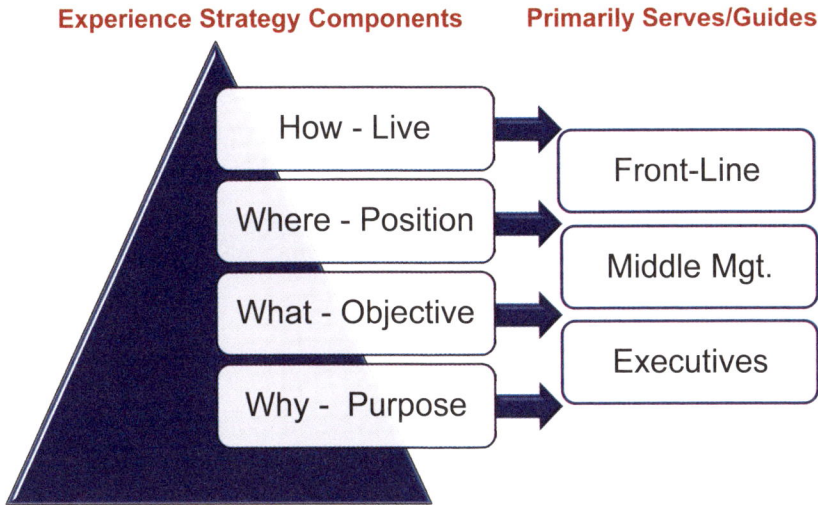

Experience Strategy Components   **Primarily Serves/Guides**

Experience Strategy Components	Primarily Serves/Guides
How - Live	Front-Line
Where - Position	Middle Mgt.
What - Objective	Executives
Why - Purpose	

For various levels of the organization:

- The purpose and objective articulates how CEM will help executives achieve the organization's macro goals

- The objective provides a scorecard and the position directs middle management's action and future decisions regarding service policies and touchpoint delivery

- The position and live provide guidelines that help all employees - especially front line employees – deliver touchpoints aligned with the position, Experience Strategy and Identity

Paul recognized that the final Experience Strategy needed to be condensed and encouraged the team to boil it down to a phrase that GIFT can rally around. The team came up with:

Promises accurately and courteously fulfilled

As the team was working on the phrase, Paul got a sense that they were close to what could be considered GIFT's Identity. With the phrase complete, he and the team discussed using "courteously accurate" as

151

a working Identity until a formal Identity is developed. The team liked the idea. They would focus on the phrase as their Strategy but would also use "courteously accurate" as their working Identity when needed.

Approved

Paul presented the Experience Strategy and phrase to the Executive Council (EC). The executives appreciated that each of the four components of the Strategy was applicable to all employees and that each of the three organizational levels of executive, middle management and front line could find aspects that were especially relevant to them.

Executives now know that these CEM efforts are designed to contribute to their targeted 5% year over year growth by becoming the leader in "likelihood to recommend" (Net Promoter score).

Middle management knows that they are to become the leaders in "likelihood to recommend" and that the desired service policy position is Equivalent Plus: *Most policies are the same as primary competitors while one policy is better and promoted.* This clarifies both decision-making and action – clearly identifying where policies should be and what decisions need to be made to properly position future policies.

Middle management also knows that the execution they are to manage to is Valued: *A standardized interaction that is customer-centric while advancing the organization's Values, Identity and Strategy, and the touchpoint's goal(s).* Middle management knows that there are going to be many Valued Touchpoint Workshops to deliver Valued Touchpoints and live their Touchpoint Promises.

Frontline employees know GIFT's desired Experience Position and that each of their touchpoints – whether for internal and external customers – is to meet their Touchpoint Promises.

The EC thanked Paul and the team for their work and approved the Experience Strategy.

Plan/CEM Plan

It was now time for Paul to develop GIFT's CEM Plan.

Deep Dive: Customer Experience Management Plan (CEM Plan)

A CEM Plan can include a variety of sections, similar to the sections of a business plan. In today's business world, it is productive to produce the Plan

in PowerPoint. It is easy to take the detailed Plan from the working deck and produce presentation or "story" decks to share internally.

Output of CEM Plan development should include:

1. Working PowerPoint deck. The working deck contains all of the information from which the Plan will be developed:

    a. Assessment results

    b. Answers to the Four Ss (Scope, Scale, Sequence, Success)

    c. Experience Strategy

        i. If complete, include Strategy

        ii. If the Experience Strategy is to be developed as part of the Plan, include

            1. Template

            2. Experience Strategy Opportunity/Plan Grid. Here is an example of an Opportunity/Plan Grid for a to-be developed Experience Strategy.

Opportunity	Plan
Define *Why:* Purpose of undertaking CEM aligned with macro goals	Draft to be developed in Q1 as one of Customer Council's early action items
Define *What*: Achievement – CEM's quantifiable objectives	Potential components: Culture, customer-centricity (Soft metrics from HR arena), differentiation and advocacy/loyalty (NPS). To be determined in Q1 as part of CEM Plan. Recommendation determined by Customer Council.
Define *Where*: Position of our service policies and touchpoint execution in the marketplace	To be determined in Q1 as part of CEM Plan. Recommendation determined by Customer Council.
Define *How*: Customers experience us living our Identity and Experience Strategy	To be started late in Q1 as part of CEM Plan. Customer Council to recommend task force to draft.
Approval	Recommended Experience Strategy to be presented to Executive Council 3rd Q

   d. For each of the Competencies

       i.   Objective Statements and goals

       ii. Opportunities surfaced from the Assessment

       iii. Opportunity/Plan Grid. Opportunities captured from the Assessment and their application to the Plan. This is an example Opportunity/Plan Grid for the Intelligence Competency.

Opportunity	Plan
Establish NPS committee	Establish at same time and as sub-set of Customer Council in 1st Q
Develop a reco regarding the two NPS methodologies	NPS Committee of customer experience, sales and market research to develop reco in 2nd Q
Expand distribution and understanding of NPS	NPS Committee of customer experience, sales and market research to develop reco in 2nd Q
Correlate NPS to top line revenue	To be determined using Brigman CX Correlation Formula in Q2 by NPS committee as part of CEM Plan

    iv. Plan details – this is the CEM Plan

        1. Develop a detailed Plan for a year

        2. Road map for two to three subsequent years

2. Story PowerPoint decks

    a. CEM Plan summary deck for short internal presentations

    b. CEM Plan detailed deck for thorough internal presentations

3. One-Page Implementation Matrix.

    a. At-a-glance view of status of major CEM Plan projects

    b. Each project's relationship to CEM Plan goals and objectives

    c. Includes champion, SMART goals, start date, red/yellow/green status and comments

    d. Perfect for CX team project reviews and internal update presentations. Here is a partial example.

Customer Experience Management Plan Implementation Matrix Phase 1								
Programs/Projects	Champ	SMART Objective	Leader	Start Date	Completion Date	Status (red or green)	Comments
1. Develop Experience Strategy	Jones	1.0 Draft Purpose statement and Objectives and present drafts to Customer Council	Jones	1/12/1900	1/1/1900		Draft complete and approved
		1.1 Position - Task force to be assembled from Customer Council to go through positioning exercises and define a draft Experience Position.	TBD	1/1/1900	1/3/1900		Scheduled
		1.2 Living - Task force to be assembled from Customer Council to define a draft set of "service standards."	TBD	1/1/1900	1/3/1900		Team selected and first meeting scheduled
		1.3 Approval - Experience Strategy approved by Customer Council to be presented to Board for approval	Smith	TBD	TBD		
2. Customer Council - Establish an engaged committee of one director/manager and one front line staff from customer facing and customer facing supporting departments/groups to drive CEM Plan and serve in the governance role	Jones	2.0 Educate Executive Council	Jones	1/12/1900	1/10/1900		
		2.1 Invite targeted participants	Jones	1/1/1900	Ongoing		

4. Gantt chart (timeline of project details)

    a. Developed from the Implementation Matrix

    b. Day-to-day tool of current and next steps and dependencie

ID	CEM Plan – Customer Council	Start	Finish	Duration	Jan 2014		Feb 2014		Mar 2014	
					1/5		2/2	2/9	3/2	3/9
1	Approval	1/2/2014	1/17/2014	12d						
2	Get on EC agenda	1/2/2014	1/17/2014	12d						
3	Draft PPT deck	1/2/2014	1/9/2014	6d						
4	Practice presentation	1/10/2014	1/16/2014	5d						
5	Present and gain approval	1/17/2014	1/17/2014	1d						
6	Secure Participants	1/20/2014	2/12/2014	18d						
7	Send meeting request to individual VPs	1/20/2014	1/20/2014	1d						
8	Meet, present, gain suggested Dir/Mger	1/21/2014	1/31/2014	9d						
9	Send meeting request to Dir/Mger	1/21/2014	1/31/2014	9d						
10	Meet, present, gain suggest front line	1/22/2014	2/12/2014	16d						
11	Successful First Meeting	2/3/2014	2/26/2014	18d						
12	Set meeting date	2/3/2014	2/26/2014	18d						
13	Develop agenda	2/3/2014	2/21/2014	15d						
14	Distribute agenda	2/21/2014	2/21/2014	1d						
15	Conduct first meeting	2/26/2014	2/26/2014	1d						
16	Charter	2/12/2014	3/10/2014	19d						
17	Develop template and examples	2/12/2014	2/26/2014	11d						
18	Hand out at first meeting	2/27/2014	2/27/2014	1d						
19	Finalize first version at 2nd meeting	3/10/2014	3/10/2014	1d						

Note: Examples of many of the forms used are available at www. TouchpointPower.com/resources. For GIFT's entire CEM Plan and interactive versions of the forms for developing a Plan, see the TOUCHPOiNT POWER Toolbox.

Paul's CEM Plan takes shape

An early step was for Paul to establish objective statements and goals for each of the Three Competencies:

- Identity
  - A. **Objective statement.** Define our Identity (the desired perception of GIFT in the mind of our customer) and live our Identity across each customer touchpoint.
  - B. **Goal.** Launch Identity definition program within three months. Complete it, including the entire Identity Pyramid, within nine months and within a $150,000 budget.

- Intelligence
  - A. **Objective statement.** Advance our Experience Strategy through getting the right information to the right people at the right time.
  - B. **Goal.** Establish voice of customer (VOC) and voice of internal customer (VOIC) macro metrics benchmarks within two months of hiring a project manager. Launch first customer listening post within three months of hiring

155

an project manager, adding one new listening post per month for the following three months.

- Consistency

    A. **Objective statement.** Solve the core customer experience problem of inconsistency by establishing a structure for the ongoing ability to standardize touchpoints to be customer-centric while achieving our Experience Strategy and delivering our Identity.

    B. **Goal.** Launch a Valued Touchpoint Workshop pilot within two months of hiring a project manager, adding one new VTW pilot per month for the following three months.

Based on his Opportunity/Plan Grid, Paul then laid out the Plan's primary components for each of the Competencies:

- Identity

    □ **Define.** Getting Executive Council approval to launch a comprehensive program with an external vendor to determine GIFT's Identity.

    □ **Live.** In collaboration with human resources (HR), getting Identity to live internally:

        ▽ Employee engagement

            ○ Providing updates to the Executive Council every 60 – 90 days

            ○ Establishing a "Customer Council." This cross-functional group of a front line staff and a manager from each customer-facing group that meets periodically for the purpose of:

                ✓ Reviewing customer issues surfaced through customer-facing employees for both solutions and root cause

                ✓ Reviewing VOC and VOIC for alerts and action planning opportunities

                ✓ Once available, review alerts for root cause

Hank Brigman

- ✓ Consolidating departmental metrics into a standard set of customer and CEM performance metrics

- ✓ Serving as the governance level for Valued Touchpoint Workshops

- ○ Working with HR to:

  - Establish a group of employees charged with bringing the Identity (once defined) to life internally

  - Develop an internal recognition and reward system for living the Identity, Competencies and Touchpoint Promises

- ○ Working with a series of marketing interns to:

  - Develop an internal communication plan

  - Execute the communication plan

- ■ Intelligence

  - ☐ Working with the Customer Council, establish a CEM Dashboard

  - ☐ Establishing Net Promoter score (NPS) as GIFT's macro customer relationship metric and correlating it to top-line revenue

  - ☐ Establishing an internal teamwork/cooperation metric to address teamwork and silo issues

  - ☐ Establishing listening posts along the journeys of GIFT's primary channels/customers at key touchpoints identified from the Assessment

    - ▽ Immediately following onboarding of a new Enterprise client and at the one year anniversary

    - ▽ Following onboarding new accounting firm reseller partner

    - ▽ Three months post registration of a Small Biz product

157

      ▽ Two months prior to the start of a strategic partner's (major office supply retailers) annual planning process and immediately after the process is completed

    ☐ Developing the ability to surface and expeditiously act on alerts as a result of customer feedback through listening posts, sales, customer service or VOC

    ☐ Providing customer facing team members with feedback on their individual performance from both external and internal customers

- Consistency

    ☐ Piloting four Valued Touchpoint Workshops (VTW) in the United States

    ☐ Basing additional U.S. Workshops on results from Intelligence efforts

    ☐ Incorporating Identity and relevant Intelligence results into VTWs

    ☐ Launching pilot Workshops in other countries

Rant: Focus on the Basics, not Wows!

A key to success of a CEM Plan is to be realistic regarding the current situation and where to start. Work to become really good at the basics before jumping to "adding value." So many companies I work with have language about exceeding expectations or "wowing" customers when they don't even deliver the basics well. Focus on consistently delivering Valued Touchpoints around your product or service, especially when customers:

- Inquire
- Consider
- Purchase
- Receive
- Pay for
- Use
- Comment
- Post
- Review

A July 2010 Harvard Business Review article, "Stop Trying to Delight Your Customers," provides a number of statistics from customer calls to customer service that support the article's title.

To me, the most poignant statistic is that customers are four times more likely to become disloyal than loyal as a result of a service touchpoint.

Yikes! Given a chance to engage customers and address an opportunity, many businesses actually fail miserably.

Secret: Focus on getting great at customer service, experience and touchpoint basics before investing in value-added efforts.

In your personal relationships, sending a gift won't make up for not returning calls, being late or failing on other basic common courtesies. The same holds for business relationships. Throwing great parties, providing sports tickets, offering staff training, etc., won't get you the bang you are seeking if you don't deliver on the expected basics.

Truth: Transitioning personal or professional relationships to a state of loyalty takes time and actions that prove that you can and will consistently deliver the basics well.

Paul was now ready to move to implementation.

Plan/Summary
A plan to deliver a value chain

At its core, the CEM Plan's purpose is geared to achieve the Experience Strategy through building the Three Competencies and delivering on the Touchpoint Principle. In doing so, the Plan will establish a Touchpoint Structure, solve the core experience problem and deliver the benefits of the Touchpoint Structure Value Chain.

The Touchpoint Principle:

The ability to get and keep desired customers and employees is enhanced by consistently delivering Valued Touchpoints

Touchpoint Structure Value Chain™

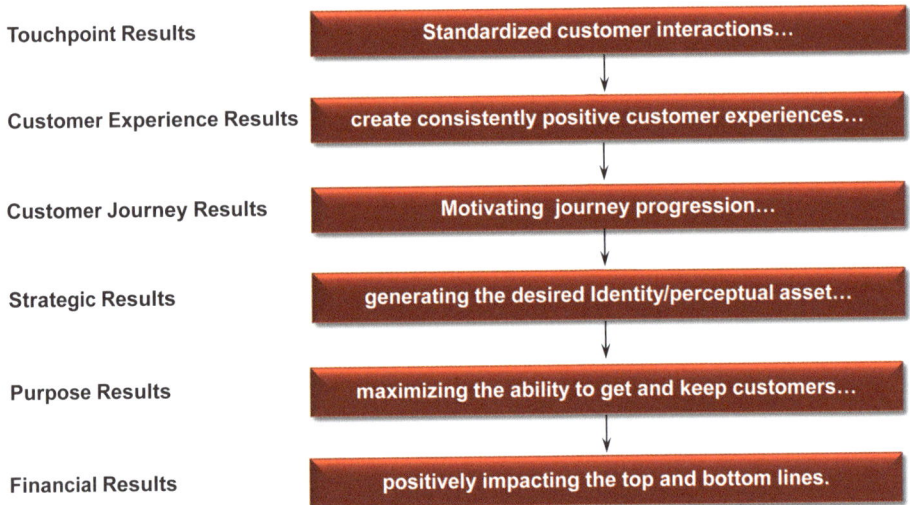

Touchpoint Results	Standardized customer interactions...
Customer Experience Results	create consistently positive customer experiences...
Customer Journey Results	Motivating journey progression...
Strategic Results	generating the desired Identity/perceptual asset...
Purpose Results	maximizing the ability to get and keep customers...
Financial Results	positively impacting the top and bottom lines.

Key points

- An Experience Strategy is made up of:

    - **Purpose (why).** Why the organization is undertaking CEM – which organizational goal does CEM efforts support/drive?

    - **Objective (what).** What is CEM to accomplish?

    - **Position (where).**
        - ▽ Where is the current state Experience Position?
        - ▽ How does it align with the Brand/Offering Position and the positions of key competitors?
        - ▽ Where is the desired state Experience Position?

    - **Live (how).** How to design and deliver touchpoints (guidelines often called "service standards")?

- The Experience Strategy template is:

    To help drive our _____ (*why* – the purpose tied to a macro organizational strategy/objective) our Experience Strategy is to _____ (*what* it is to quantifiably accomplish) through positioning our service policies as _____ and our touchpoint execution as _____

(*where* we are positioned) and consistently delivering our
_____ (*how* we live our Identity and
Experience Strategy across customer touchpoints).

- Follow the Experience Strategy positioning questions and maps to determine the current position and desired state position (where)

- An Experience Strategy boiled down to a word or phrase should align with the organization's Identity

- The components of a Customer Experience Management Plan (CEM Plan) can include:

  - Working deck

  - Story decks – summary and detailed

  - One-Page Implementation Matrix

  - Gantt chart

- For each Competency, develop objective statements and goals

- Focus on getting consistently good at the basics before attempting to add value

Chapter 9: Model Step 3, Operationalize

Building a Touchpoint Structure through Ongoing Workshops that Create Value for Both Customer and Organization

Operationalize

Operationalize
A multi-faceted implementation plan

Paul would work first on hiring his staff and concurrently building the Three Customer-Centricity Competencies:

- **Identity.** Launch a Customer Council and define Identity.
- **Intelligence.** Establish macro customer and internal metrics and correlate the macro metric to top-line revenue.
- **Consistency.** Pilot Value Touchpoint Workshops.

Operationalize/Hiring
Hiring staff to meet the needs of the CEM Plan

Paul hired Otto and Lucy. Lucy was a researcher with strong analytical skills and Otto was a project manager who was also a Six Sigma Black Belt.

Otto was to start by setting up the Valued Touchpoint Workshop pilots. He would serve as workshop facilitator. Lucy would work with market research to set up the macro metrics and listening posts.

Black Belt

A Black Belt is a Six Sigma team leader responsible for implementing process improvement projects within the business to increase customer satisfaction levels and business productivity. Black Belts are knowledgeable and skilled in the use of the Six Sigma methodology and tools.

Black Belts have typically completed four weeks of Six Sigma training, and have demonstrated mastery of the subject matter through the completion of project(s) and an exam.

Black Belts coach Green Belts and receive coaching and support from Master Black Belts

Source: www.isixsigma.com

Paul was also promised a communication intern by Maggie to help with employee engagement efforts.

Secret: The skills needed on your CEM team should be based on your CEM Plan.

Operationalize/Correlation
Early wins, win

As with all new efforts, Paul knew that early wins are huge. One of his early efforts would be to correlate CEM to financial metrics in order to meet the Executive Council's direction to measure success in financial terms (hard metrics).

Previous short-term based decisions leave a negative legacy

For Paul, correlating NPS to financial metrics was especially important. The Audit uncovered that GIFT had changed some of its customer service policies over recent years. Each specific change in customer service policies had been championed by Boris, Chief Financial Officer. Most of these changes were adopted by the EC late in a year when GIFT was behind its financial "plan" and needed to make up ground to meet its financial projections. While these policy changes didn't always facilitate meeting financial objectives, the reduction in service did frustrate both customers and employees.

Paul realized that VOC and VOIC results would shine a negative light on these changes. However, Paul knew that the survey results wouldn't answer Boris's typical question, "so what does that translate into financially?" In order to get the powerful CFO to support his initiatives, he would need to get CEM into Boris's language – money.

Correlating Net Promoter score to revenue

Since GIFT had captured NPS three times over the prior 18 months, Paul was able to apply Brigman's CX Correlation Formula™ to the results.

The formula provides the ability to correlate a one point movement in Net Promoter score (NPS) to top line revenue.

Paul was thrilled with the outcome. It turns out that a one point movement in GIFT's NPS correlates to $1.5 million dollars in top-line revenue. Paul looked forward to sharing this with the EC, and especially with Boris.

> Note: see the Resources Section for Brigman's CX Correlation Formula™.

Operationalize/Identity
Identity – a key strategic component

Paul knew that getting the EC's approval to define GIFT's Identity required educating EC members. He needed to bring them up to speed on what an Identity is, its strategic importance, and the options for defining an Identity. During a one-on-one with Maggie, Paul explained his plan for introducing the Identity topic, and the two options for GIFT to develop their Identity. Maggie put Paul on the next EC meeting agenda.

Critical two assets and their journeys defined

Paul started by engaging the EC in mapping out the steps GIFT goes through to produce its software, a critical asset. Together they captured the primary steps as:

Functional Specs → Write Code → Test/QA → De-Bug → Launch → Asset: Product

They then mapped out the steps or experiences of the customer journey for their Enterprise product. Once complete, Paul introduced the concept that this journey created a second critical asset – the perception of GIFT in the mind of the customer.

Market → Sale → Install → Account → Train & Service → Perceptual Asset

Combined, these two assets serve to establish GIFT's Identity. Paul noted how each step of the product journey worked in conjunction with the previous and next step to generate the specified product and that the same needed to be said of the customer journey. The fact that GIFT had not clearly defined the perceptual asset it sought to generate hindered its ability to establish a specific and advantageous Identity.

Secret: Know the steps and experiences of these journeys prior to engaging executives in this exercise. It is not uncommon that executives in large organizations aren't aware of some of the specific steps in journeys. Let the executives define the steps but be prepared to assist if they stumble.

With an understanding of the two journeys and their related assets, Paul laid out two options for defining GIFT's Identity – the desired perceptual asset.

Option 1. Economical
The economical option involved hiring a brand consultant who would conduct an assessment, develop an Identity Brief based on findings, and then conduct a workshop to define the Identity. The assessment would include some internal interviews and review of internal, agency and external secondary data.

Option 2. Thorough
The Thorough approach would involve significantly more primary research.

- This option would involve a defendable examination of:
  - Current brand Identity
  - Brand Identity of competitors
  - Identify "white space" among competitors (white space is the space competitors don't occupy)
  - Desirable Identity within that white space
  - Relevance of that Identity to organization's customers
  - Delta between current Identity and potential Identity

White Space
An under-served business market or undeveloped product category

Source: www. Doubletongued.org

□ Effort needed to achieve that Identity

□ The value of achieving that Identity

□ Relevance of potential Identity to primary target market(s)

- Clear implementation plan to go from current to desired Identity

The investment for Option 1 would be in the $30,000 - $50,000 range while Option 2 would run $120,000 - $170,000.

Paul explained that the competitive information is especially important as Identity is a key to positioning, and as such, must be determined against the competitive set.

There was a consensus from the EC on the need to develop its Identity. The discussion revolved around which option to apply. As the discussion progressed, Paul resisted the desire to jump in, letting the discussion take its own course except when asked a direct question.

Maggie heard the opinions from many of the group, and then offered hers. While acknowledging that dollars were tight, she viewed developing their Identity as a foundational investment that would be integral to all that they did moving forward. She shared that their efforts to differentiate via customer-centricity needed to be built on solid foundations, of which their Identity is a key. She voiced her desire for the thorough option.

As the discussion continued, Boris again returned to his perception of the challenge of quantifying the financial impact of these efforts and his concern with the overall cost of making this move.

Despite Boris's points, EC members aligned with Maggie's desire to invest in the thorough option.

Secret: When possible and practical, give decision makers two options from which to choose. You get what you need no matter which option they select. In sales, this is known as the "either or" close.

RFP to get to the right vendor

Paul and Lucy set out to find and select a vendor for GIFT's Identity project. They developed an RFP and submitted it to eight firms they found through online research and referrals.

Note: Developing your Identity is a complex and dynamic process with many different possible methodologies to get to the same or similar result. *TOUCHPOiNT POWER* is not the vehicle for a thorough deep dive into how an Identity is developed.

167

Operationalize/Identity/Research

A vendor was selected. Paul shared the Experience Strategy process and output with the chosen vendor. The vendor found the boiled-down phrase of *"Promises accurately and courteously fulfilled"* insightful as they launched their research.

Identity research insightful

Paul found the results from the vendor's research insightful. The research uncovered that the bulk of GIFT's buyers were in the accounting and/or technology fields. Both fields require a high degree of accuracy from their professionals. Interestingly, there currently weren't any competitors claiming an accurate and detail oriented related Identity that accounting and technology customers would find attractive. This was identified in the research as white space that GIFT could claim.

Operationalize/Identity/Pyramid
Workshop produces solid Identity Pyramid

The research played a large part in building GIFT's Identity Pyramid. The vendor then facilitated a series of workshops with a diverse group sliced from throughout the organization. The Identity workshop was intense and produced Structural Foundations of GIFT's Identity Pyramid that resonated with all involved.

Foundations

> 4. Mission: Accurately deliver help and value with every customer touch
>
> 3. Vision: Globally available accounting software of choice for detailed oriented individuals & organizations
>
> 2. Identity: Promises accurately and courteously fulfilled
>
> 1. Values: Fast, Fair, Fastidious

Note: Transitioning an organization to a new Identity often requires a plan for how to get employees to make a significant shift in thoughts, beliefs and/or perceptions. It is only through a stepped process that behavior can then exhibit significant change. The *TOUCHPOiNT POWER* Toolbox provides a useful tool to plan and manage such a significant transition.

Equivalent Plus position decided

With the Pyramid complete, the Identity workshop moved on to define the policy on which to build GIFT's Equivalent Plus Brand/Offering position – the position chosen during the Experience Position mapping exercise. Through the workshop it was decided that GIFT would begin guaranteeing accuracy. While accuracy was somewhat implied by all in the market, no one really staked it out and owned that Identity attribute. Guaranteed accuracy would be GIFT's single "plus" policy that was better than the competition and promoted.

The EC and all of those involved with the workshop were thrilled with the output.

Operationalize/Intelligence
Intelligence – much to do

Paul recognized that it would be a long-term process to get the right information to the right people at the right time. The CEM Plan called for Intelligence efforts to start on three fronts:

- Net Promoter score (NPS) – solidify as the metric for measuring the health of the overall customer relationship.

- Listening posts – where GIFT is already listening or where it is easy to listen, develop a coordinated process for gathering, analyzing, sharing and acting on NPS and its VOC (voice of the customer) data.

- Voice of Internal Customer (VOIC) – launch efforts to gain insights into reasons for departmental cooperation challenges via voice of internal customer surveys. VOIC to look at both infrastructure – the policies, procedures and systems by which staff are required to operate – and the individual staff themselves. Key will be to establish a VOIC macro metric that provides insight into the overall health of colleague teamwork and cooperation.

The three metrics efforts would produce intelligence to be integrated into:

1. Immediate action – generating alerts that drive action within 24 hours
2. Planning – both strategic and tactical
3. Individual feedback – customer and colleague feedback on individual employee performance
4. Valued Touchpoint Workshops (VTW)

Lucy, Paul's new hire, would spearhead his team's Intelligence efforts.

Mini Rant: Starting from Scratch – If We Only Could

Ideally, all companies would start their Intelligence efforts or the Measure step of the Touchpoint Principle Implementation Model from scratch. There is typically significant garbage in and around current data and collection methods – garbage around who we ask, what we ask, and what we do (and don't do) with the information. There is also plenty of garbage around the political nature of legacy measures – the politics of those internally and externally responsible for the measures and related work, and those who use the measures for historical trending. It is not uncommon that we actually tie bad measures to key dashboards and bonuses/compensation.

Few organizations have the luxury of actually starting from scratch. You will need to develop your Intelligence and Measure process and programs as appropriate and given what will work within your organization.

Persona

A persona is a fictional character that communicates the primary characteristics of a group of users, identified and selected as a key target through use of segmentation data, across the company in a usable and effective manner.

Source: www.foviance.com

Note: Segmentation is a key factor in any research. Since establishing segmentation and/ or personas is highly specific to each organization, it is not covered in great detail here in TOUCHPOiNT POWER. It is important to understand the segments or personas of your customers that are most profitable and those that provide the greatest, or potentially the greatest, Lifetime Customer Value. To make segmentation work well, establish a standard set of segmentation questions to apply to all/most customer research.

Lucy, a bit different, but a good fit

Paul met with Lucy to work out their Intelligence plan. Lucy had purple hair, tattoos, piercings and a taste for music from groups he had never heard of. Paul hired her because she appeared highly competent. In working with her, Paul noticed that she had a sharp attention to detail, research acumen and the ability to interpret data in a meaningful way. While Paul found these attributes valuable, the quality that he most admired was her utter fearlessness. In their short time together he noticed that she had the facts and that she found strength and power in that. Paul needed facts. He knew he was going to need facts as a way of attempting to override politics – and to speak truth to power.

Paul outlined how he wanted Lucy to lead the research component and its contribution to quantifying CEM, the Valued Touchpoint Workshops and resultant customer and internal touchpoints.

Operationalize/Intelligence/NPS

Lucy was well versed in Net Promoter score (NPS). The research aspect was well documented and based on a single question: How likely are you to recommend GIFT?

A standard follow-up question to NPS

Lucy advocated a follow-up open-ended question around "why" the NPS rating. She explained to Paul that this VOC serves as exploratory research to surface issues and to guide future research. Additionally, she planned to develop standard demographic questions to enable consistent and meaningful segmentation of data. Segmentation questions and customer identifiers will also enable her to perform valuable regression analysis correlating NPS to various customer attributes and performance.

Exploratory Research

Investigation into a problem or situation which provides insights to the researcher. The research is meant to provide details where a small amount of information exists. It may use a variety of methods such as trial studies, interviews, group discussions, experiments, or other tactics for the purpose of gaining information.

Source: www.business dictionary.com

171

Operationalize/Intelligence/VOIC

Lucy establishes Net Teamwork™ score as VOIC macro metric

While NPS is well-established as a macro customer relationship metric, Paul and Lucy weren't aware of a corresponding metric to measure internal cooperation and teamwork. Lucy set out to develop this important metric and came up with what she called; Net Teamwork score (NTS).

Regression Analysis

Statistical approach to forecasting change in a dependent variable (sales revenue, for example) on the basis of change in one or more independent variables (population and income, for example).

Source: www.business dictionary.com

Designed after NPS, NTS is also based on a single question with a follow-up open-ended question:

How cooperative is _____ (department or individual)?

Extremely Cooperative   Not Cooperative at all

    10   9   8   7   6   5   4   3   2   1   0

On the 0 – 10 point scale, the responses break down as follows:

    9, 10 = Partner
    7, 8 = Passive
    0-6 = Loner

As with NPS, the percentage of Partners less the percentage of Loner equals a Net Teamwork score (NTS).

The NTS question would be followed-up with the open-ended question: Why?

Operationalize/Intelligence/Listening Posts

Three initial listening posts to gather VOC

Lucy's plan for listening posts was to start:

- Where GIFT was already listening
- Where listening was easy to implement and would provide value
- At the experiences to be covered by the Valued Touchpoint Workshop pilots

All would include both VOC and VOIC research.

Based on where GIFT was already listening and where listening was easy to implement and provide value, Lucy considered:

- Conferences and training where surveys were already being distributed to ascertain the effectiveness of the speaker or training

- Call center where the system had Interactive Voice Response (IVR) survey functionality

- The experiences chosen for each of the Valued Touchpoint Workshop (VTW) pilots

360 degree reviews of all involved

It was Lucy's hope that those employees involved would embrace post-event 360-degree reviews. Her idea was to survey all those involved in those experiences. For instance, at the conclusion of a conference, a survey would be sent to all teammates to rate Net Teamwork score of those they worked with on the conference. Results would be aggregated and shared with individuals and their managers.

Truth: Honest feedback from one's peers improves behavior.

Based on results from the Assess Audit, three areas Lucy considered:

- Immediately following onboarding of a new Enterprise client and at the one year anniversary

- Following onboarding new accounting firm reseller partner

- Three months post registration of a Small Biz product

- Two months prior to the start of a strategic partner's (major office supply retailers) annual planning process and immediately after the process is completed

IVR (Interactive Voice Response)

An automated telephone information system that speaks to the caller with a combination of fixed voice menus and data extracted from databases in real time. The caller responds by pressing digits on the telephone or speaking words or short phrases.

Source: www.pcmag.com

Lucy needed to build listening posts as part of an overarching VOC research program, while also meeting the specific intelligence needs at that listening post. She would structure a few standard segmentation questions for data continuity across listening posts. She would also craft specific and unique segmentation questions for surveys as needed.

To practice what the CEM team was preaching, Lucy planned to seek input from each member of the Valued Touchpoint Workshop pilots

360-degree review

Performance-appraisal data collected from 'all around' an employee his or her peers, subordinates, supervisors, and sometimes, from internal and external customers. Its main objective usually is to assess training and development needs and to provide competence-related information for succession planning not promotion or pay increase. Also called multi-rater assessment, multi-source assessment, multi-source feedback.

Source: www.businessdictionary.com

— the Touchpoint Teams — to uncover what intelligence would be valuable and actionable in the Workshop pilots.

Operationalize/Intelligence/Alerts & Planning

From intelligence to action

An important goal of Intelligence efforts is to incorporate results into action through alerts and into planning. Both Otto and Lucy planned to work with those involved to set the rules for what constitutes an alert, where the alert goes and how to close the loop.

A second goal of the Intelligence efforts is to establish a system for packaging and communicating insights in a way that they are valuable in departmental and organizational planning. This helps build plans that are more customer-centric and helps reduce inconsistency.

Otto and Lucy decided to suggest to Paul that the development of the VOC and VOIC programs should be their own Valued Touchpoint Workshop pilots. This would ensure that the process for gathering and distributing the results of these important macro metrics would be customer-centric — easy for customers while creating data and systems valued by those served internally.

Operationalize/Consistency/Engagement

Paul knew that employee engagement would be a key to the success of building the Consistency Competency.

Operationalize/Consistency/Engagement/ Customer Council

Customer Council a source of potential early wins

Another early win Paul wanted to focus on was helping to improve communication and handoffs along customer journeys. Paul's CEM coach recommended establishing a Customer Council — ongoing meetings between the managers and a customer-facing employee from each of the disparate customer-facing departments or groups.

The coach explained that these simple meetings often surface low-hanging fruit for either customer touchpoint or internal efficiency improvements. The Customer Council would also serve as the source for the governance level of Valued Touchpoint Workshops. More on governance soon.

Deep Dive: Customer Council

A Customer Council (or whatever you call it) is typically made up of a single manager and one customer-facing employee from each of the disparate customer-facing departments/groups and those serving customer-facing departments/groups. The Council meets regularly to improve internal cooperation, communication and metrics, and to resolve issues with customers and touchpoints.

> Note: In smaller companies, the Customer Council can be made up of individuals responsible for customer touchpoints.

Secret: Position employee participation on the Council and the Workshops as a development opportunity for future leaders. This enables the Council to secure participation of motivated individuals who will work hard and smart to produce positive results.

Holding Customer Council meetings in a "customer room"

In her book, *Chief Customer Officer: Getting Past Lip Service to Passionate Action©* (Jeanne Bliss, Publisher Jossey-Bass 2006), Jeanne Bliss promotes the advantages of establishing a "customer room." A customer room is a conference room where customer touchpoints are posted. As communication touchpoints are developed, they are posted in the room, adding to those already deployed in the marketplace and posted in the room.

Organize the room along Customer Relationship Journey stages: Awareness, Knowledge, Consideration, Selection, Satisfaction, Loyalty, and Advocacy. This helps those involved in developing and deploying touchpoints see the other touchpoints customers are encountering in and around the one(s) they are developing.

A customer room enables staff to "see" the holistic customer journey and the totality of the communication targeting customers. This can help improve the

175

continuity and effectiveness of both the visual and message components of the organization's marketing communication and Identity.

A customer room is a great idea, and if it can be done, is the perfect place for the Customer Council to meet.

Truth: Your Customer Council – in fact almost any team – can benefit from a charter. A charter sets out the scope, personnel and objectives of the group.

> Note: A charter template, Doc # 510, Customer Council Charter Template, can be downloaded at www.TouchpointPower.com/members.

Operationalize/Consistency/Engagement/Customer Council/Meeting Agenda
Enthusiasm for the Council

Understanding the importance of this group, Paul decided that he would facilitate these meetings. He took the Council through the agenda during the inaugural meeting including the CEM 101 PowerPoint presentation. There was enthusiasm from the group, especially from front-line staff. They were excited that they would have an opportunity to truly impart changes that would benefit customers as well as their day-to-day work. After the meeting, individuals stayed around talking, asking questions and communicating how much these efforts were needed.

Concerns about executive commitment

The biggest concern raised during and after the meetings was the executive's commitment to what was needed to truly impact change. Most had seen programs and initiatives come and go. They had heard previous talk from executives about how important the customer is but saw little action behind the words.

How are we going to pay for it?

The second concern was somewhat related. Most front-line staff felt that the changes that needed to be made were technological or other changes that required significant budget. They all knew how tight funds were and voiced concern that there wasn't much that could actually be done without budget.

Getting them focused on what they *could* change

Paul's CEM coach had prepped him that this would be a voiced concern. He shared their frustration with the problems they faced. However, he communicated that there was much that could be done spending little or no money. Paul used specific examples surfaced through the Assessment of opportunities to improve customer experiences by improving internal handoffs and communication – things that didn't cost any money.

Paul's key point was to work together to demonstrate and prove the effectiveness of CEM by focusing on what they could control. This would ensure ongoing support. And once that was accomplished, they could build solid business cases for making practical capital investments that would provide quantifiable and positive returns.

Each meeting of the Council was to follow the same agenda:

- Old business
  - ☐ Review/status of outstanding action items
- Current business
  - ☐ Front-line – what are you hearing since our last meeting?
  - ☐ How can we improve the customer experience and/or internal efficiencies around/as we deal with that issue?
  - ☐ What is the core problem that generates that issue?
  - ☐ How do we address the core problem?
  - ☐ What are the metrics telling us?
- New business

Operationalize/Consistency/Engagement/Customer Council/ Dashboard

Metrics bring insight into dysfunctional nature of cooperation

After four or five meetings, Paul moved on to metrics. He asked each manager to bring the customer and internal metrics their group or department tracked. The new business section of the meeting was expanded so that each department/group could present their metrics. Each covered why they tracked the specific metric, what the metric laddered up to and how each drove change or improvements.

A goal was to uncover where metrics were driving behavior that hindered positive customer experiences within a department or negatively impacted another department's efforts.

First-Call Resolution & Talk Time

In customer relationship management (CRM), first-call resolution is properly addressing the customer's need the first time they call, thereby eliminating the need for the customer to follow up with a second call. Talk time (the average time an agent spends on each call) is a common call center performance metric. In general, fast talk time averages are desirable. However, fast talk time averages accompanied by poor first-call resolution rates are a sign that customer calls are not being answered satisfactorily.

Call center managers carefully monitor follow-up calls because in addition to being an indication of customer dissatisfaction, follow-up calls create an overall increased call volume which, in turn, requires more agents. In general, a call center manager will accept an increase in talk time, as long as the first call resolution rate increases as well.

Source: www.searchcrm.com

Paul wanted to use the metrics presentations as a basis for establishing a customer experience dashboard that would help drive a more holistic view of the customer journey.

What they uncovered was shocking. A couple of examples stood out:

- The representative from finance reported that they tracked customer bad debt and defaults. The rep from Sales responded that Finance's focus on bad debt and resultant practice of being overly restrictive on new accounting firm resellers' credit was hindering sales and the positive experiences of new resellers.

- The call center rep discussed their primary metric of call time. They had just started tracking first-call resolution, which was significantly below industry standards. The rep from Sales reported that it was common to receive calls from customers who could not get their issues addressed by customer service or technical support. These calls by frustrated customers to sales reps took the reps away from their primary purpose – selling.

- Technical Support reported tracking a high attrition/drop-out rate of customers on the lowest tier of support. There was a high degree of frustration in customer service because they couldn't do anything to resolve the high attrition rate due to GIFT's policy of charging Tier 3 support customers for phone support. The rep from sales confirmed the frustration Tier 3 support customers had with having to pay for phone support and the time and effort it took for sales reps to deal with those customers and issues.

The group was amazed at how the issues they measured contributed to disjointed customer experiences. Sharing metrics clearly highlighted the negative impact different departments can have on both customers and their colleagues in sales. Most in the group had no idea that their sales reps spent so much time addressing customer issues rather than selling. The group discussed the benefit to the business of reducing customer issues so that the sales force could devote additional time to building business and how that would help everyone at GIFT.

Intersection – Customer Council and Intelligence

Paul brought in Otto and Lucy to bring the Customer Council up to speed on developments around customer relationship and internal teamwork macro metrics and listening posts. The two of them were to work with the Council on developing a customer experience (CX) dashboard that would get each department better focused on their impact on the holistic customer journey.

As a starting point, the dashboard included:

- Net Promoter score (NPS)

- VOIC macro metric – Net Teamwork score (NTS)

- New customers this period (total and percentage of total customers)

- Lost customers this period (total and percentage of total customers)

- Net customers (total and percentage to prior year and period)

- Number of customers on each support tier

The Council's initial dashboard:

Metric	This Period	Prior Period	Delta	% Change
NPS	5	6	-1	-16.6%
NTS	11	9	2	22.2%
New Customers	72	70	2	2.9%
Lost Customers	65	61	4	-6.6%
Net Customers	7	9	-2	-22.2
Tier 1 Support	1289	1280	9	0.7%
Tier 2 Support	1819	1814	5	0.3%
Tier 3 Support	2329	2409	-80	-3.3

Operationalize/Consistency/Engagement/
Internal Communication

Internal communication builds understanding and support

Paul sat down with Sarah, the communications intern assigned to his team. Entering her senior year in the fall at a local university, Sarah wanted some relevant work experience prior to graduation. Sarah was available for only three months this summer and he knew that there was a lot to accomplish within that timeframe.

Paul walked Sarah through the CEM Plan and CEM 101 presentations to bring her up to speed. Paul was pleased with her quick grasp and relevant questions. With an understanding of his team's charge, Paul asked Sarah to develop a proposed communications plan with an understanding that she would build out the needed infrastructure for her replacement to implement in the Fall.

A week later Sarah presented Paul with a PowerPoint overview with supporting documentation that included a detailed Gantt Chart. Paul liked her work. Recognizing that she was a bit overly aggressive in her assumption of what could realistically be accomplished within the time frame, Paul helped her pare it down to a more practical and workable plan.

Gantt Chart

Type of bar-chart that shows both the scheduled and completed work over a period. A time-scale is given on the chart's horizontal axis and each activity is shown as a separate horizontal rectangle (bar) whose length is proportional to the time required (or taken) for the activity's completion. In project planning, these charts show start and finish dates, critical and non-critical activities, slack time, and predecessor-successor relationships. Also called chronogram, it was invented in 1917 by the US engineer and a scientific-management pioneer, Henry L. Gantt (1861-1919).

Source: www.businessdictionary.com

In the end, the plan included:

- A brand for the CEM plan. It was to be called "North Star" based on a combination of the CEM Plan and GIFT's customers providing the guiding light on the journey to customer-centricity.

- Posters

- Intranet use for videos and presentations and their distribution to each department

- Periodic video newsletters and announcements and their distribution to each department

■ Coordination with HR on the Identity and recognition/reward program rollout

Operationalize/Consistency/Engagement/HR

Paul was fortunate to have an outstanding relationship with Graham, the head of human resources (HR). A likable guy who retained a heavy Scottish accent despite leaving Edinburgh following university, Graham was totally onboard with Paul's plan and embraced his department's role. Creative, Graham was especially interested in coming up with a celebration and reward program for the new Identity.

Operationalize/Consistency/VTW

Selecting the right experience to pilot is critical

During the Assessment, low-hanging fruit was identified. It is from this list that initial project(s) or pilot(s) for Valued Touchpoint Workshop (VTW) would be chosen.

Deep Dive: Selecting Valued Touchpoint Workshops to Pilot

Generating early wins is typically critical. Look to experiences or processes that have the potential to demonstrate positive results:

■ With Finance – moving important financial needles

■ With employees – improving work life and getting positive internal word-of-mouth

■ With the CEM team – generating a feeling of momentum and success

■ With the chief executive – giving him/her the business case for scaling and further investing in CEM

There are a number of additional factors important in choosing a pilot or pilots:

■ **Linier.** Choose an experience that is linier in its execution. In other words, the experience follows a typical path and has a natural beginning and end.

■ **Impacts revenue.** Choose an experience that has the opportunity to deliver a significant ROI, especially one that drives revenue.

■ **Engages supporters.** Choose an experience that engages the departments and/or individuals that support CEM efforts and avoid experiences that rely strongly on departments headed by those in opposition.

181

Pilots to consider include onboarding new customers (B2B), the sales process (B2B, B2C), fulfillment (B2B, B2C), returns (B2B, B2C), complaints (B2B, B2C), and customer training/events (B2B).

Rule: Choose your Valued Touchpoint Workshop pilots carefully.

Secret: It is typically constructive to avoid call center calls as pilots. Incoming call center calls are typically not linier – they can branch off into many different directions. Achieve wins and build Workshop competence prior to tackling Workshops focused on the call center.

Rant: Call Centers Are NOT an Expense – Put Them in Sales & Marketing

If you have a call center, chances are it is viewed through a single financial lens – expense. Leaders of call centers typically rise up through operations and are charged with minimizing the expense of their department.

Remember in the July 7, 2010 Harvard Business Review article by Matthew Dixon, Karen Freeman, and Nicholas Toman, *Stop Trying to Delight Your Customers,* customers are four times more likely to become **disloyal** rather than **loyal** after a service touchpoint. Think about that. As your customers engage with your organization, the interaction is typically so bad that they are more likely to become disloyal rather than loyal. What does this say about most call center touchpoints?

Call centers often suffer from, "what gets measured gets done." A bane of customer experience efforts is the call center metric "call time." A knee jerk reaction is that less call time means less time for the reps on the phone and fewer reps in seats, saving money. An intuitive analysis comes up with the quite the opposite. If reps are measured on how long they are on the phone, they will shorten calls – "what gets measured, gets done." Chances are shortened calls will not address all of the customer's issues, leading to additional calls. Additional calls mean more reps and higher costs – and an unhappy customer.

For many companies, the call center is the primary means of interacting or engaging with customers. This should be considered an area for *investment,* not an expense department. This is an opportunity to build Lifetime Customer Value.

A strategy for success?

Zappos.com is a company recognized for their amazing customer-centricity. Here is a company that invests in their customer "engagement" center (rather than call center). They don't measure call time. Not at all. Anecdotally, their longest call was over eight hours. Imagine. They train their reps to engage with customers rather than to rush them off the phone.

The fact that Zappos.com hit $1 billion U.S. in sales nine years after its 1999 launch and in 2009 was purchased by Amazon for a reported $1.2 billion U.S. certainly supports their customer focus as a viable strategy.

Call centers becoming proactive

The call center is evolving. Progressive companies are undertaking creative ways of utilizing their best call center personnel. Some are discarding the pure passive role of just accepting calls and creating teams taking proactive roles in making outbound calls. These calls can be to address service issues, reach out to lost customers, aid "go to market" strategies, etc.

As a critical opportunity to engage your customer and further establish your desired Identity – that perceptual asset in the mind of your customer – your call center should be a part of your sales and marketing organization. Remove it from operations.

Consistency – pilots to show wins and build teamwork and a critical competency

Paul and his team, with results from the Assessment and input from the Customer Council, decided to propose four pilots:

- Onboarding new Enterprise customers
- Building VOC listening posts
- Developing macro metrics (VOC and VOIC)
- Software complaints/bugs

The first pilot would be onboarding Enterprise clients, with an additional pilot starting every four weeks. This was an aggressive start that required a lot of Paul, Otto and Lucy. Especially Otto, who would be facilitating the pilots. The EC liked and approved the plan.

Kaizen
Japanese term for a gradual approach to ever higher standards in quality enhancement and waste reduction, through small but continual improvements involving everyone from the chief executive to the lowest level workers. Popularized by Mosaki Imai in his books 'Kaizen: The Key To Japan's Competitive Success.'

Source: www.businessdictionary.com

Embracing moving from the expense side to the revenue side of the ledger

Otto, Paul's new hire to facilitate Valued Touchpoint Workshops (VTW), embraced the idea of these workshops. While similar conceptually

---

Kaizen Event/Blitz

A period during which a group of managers and workers work together to solve a problem or improve a particular process within a company:

A kaizen event brings together employees to examine a problem, propose solutions, and implement change.

Source:
www.dictionary.cambridge.org

---

to the Kaizen Events or Kaizens he had historically facilitated, he understood and embraced the distinctions and the much deeper dives into the "hows" of individual touchpoints. With his previous employers, he found that over time colleagues developed resentment to the sometime formal structure of Kaizens.

Otto loved the idea of engaging customers in VTW or having an employee playing the role of the "customer" when one wasn't involved. While his prior quality work had always focused on and delivered significant internal efficiencies to lower expenses, he was eager to focus on improving the revenue side of the financial equation as well.

VTW at the ready

Like Lucy, Otto was detail-oriented. In contrast, Otto was far less a free spirit and a bit more compulsive in his attention to detail. He had his facilitation tools at the ready, neatly categorized in his dark blue rolling file box. Post-its, pens, colored markers and dots all in their P-Touch labeled place, and always fully stocked. The file box had its place in his cube right next to three rolls of butcher paper. Otto was a Valued Touchpoint Workshop ready to happen.

Otto knew that the plan was to dramatically expand the scale of Workshops over time. Otto proposed that some of the senior call center supervisors could potentially serve as future facilitators. Call center supervisors were above reps but below managers in the call center hierarchy. Paul thought it a great idea and the two of them met with Mike, the head of Customer Service to float the idea.

Operationalize/Consistency/VTW/Facilitators
A partner in the head of GIFT's call centers

As the head of an expense side department, Mike was tired of the never-ending pressure to reduce costs. A large and jolly man, Mike recently joined GIFT having run the call center for a manufacturing company. It was there that he had risen through the ranks of operations by being ever more efficient. Do more with less was his charge each and every year. But Mike hadn't become cynical. He was, at his core, customer-centric. Mike recognized an opportunity to jump on an important initiative and gain visibility for himself and his department. He sought greater appreciation for his department while at the same time improving its service and efficiency.

It was determined that Otto would use the pilots to train apprentice facilitators from customer service. Politically astute, Otto pondered a future where he would manage a team of facilitators on a global basis. No more rolling blue file box for him. Yes, he liked his new job. He liked it a lot.

Deep Dive: Valued Touchpoint Workshops – THE Differentiator

Of the Three Customer-Centricity Competencies, Consistency is the differentiator. Consistency solves the core experience problem of inconsistency. It is Consistency that separates the iconic customer-centric companies for the rest. Apple is always Apple. They are consistently Apple at *every* touchpoint. McDonalds, Disney, Southwest Airlines are consistently who they are – their Identity – at each and every touchpoint.

Consistent delivery of Identity and Experience Strategy across each and every touchpoint is historically the hardest part of becoming customer-centric – that is why a Touchpoint Structure differentiates. The challenge for those aspiring to be customer-centric has

Valued Touchpoint Workshop (VTW)

A team of relevant colleagues mapping and evaluating the current state of touchpoints of an experience or journey (if a current state exists), and designing, implementing, promoting and measuring a desired state of Valued Touchpoints.

Valued Touchpoint™

A standardized interaction that is customer-centric while advancing the organization's values, Identity and strategy, and the touchpoint's goal(s).

historically been "how" – how to get an Experience Strategy and Identity to "live" at each and every touchpoint? In other words, how to close the strategy-to-touchpoint gap?

Of all of the ideas and suggestions in *TOUCHPOiNT POWER*, I believe that how to conduct VTW and getting to the granularity of the Four Valued Touchpoint Questions is the most valuable. This is the key to developing a competitive advantage that is defendable.

As your organization or department evolves, it is establishing new touchpoints on an ongoing basis that need to be developed and deployed as Valued Touchpoints. This level of detail and granularity is the hard part and why so few organizations achieve customer-centricity. Take the VTW ideas presented here, modify as needed, and apply on an ongoing basis to developing and deploying Valued Touchpoints.

Truth: The key task of operationalizing your CEM Plan is to turn inconsistent touchpoints into Valued Touchpoints through Valued Touchpoint Workshops. This process is the Consistency Competency your organization must master.

Truth: To be customer-centric, Valued Touchpoint Workshops will be launched on an ongoing basis in perpetuity.

A portion of your CEM Plan will focus on defining the logistics around Valued Touchpoint Workshops.

Secret: While Valued Touchpoint Workshops are focused on improving customer-centricity, it is a methodology/tool for closing any strategy-to-touchpoint gap.

A case for workshops

Professor Paul Nutt researched different styles used to implement strategies. Over 350 implementations were classified as:

- **Tell.** Leader announces path and tells people what to do.
- **Persuade.** Leader sells decision based on evidence and waits for support.
- **Participate.** Leader delegates action to group and waits recommendations.
- **Engage.** Leader creates awareness of gap between current and desired states and engages others in determining solutions.

The research found that Tell and Persuade were the most commonly used, while Engage turns out to be far more successful. Source: *Managing the Customer Experience,* (Prentice Hall, 2002), Shaun Smith, & Joe Wheeler.

Valued Touchpoint Workshops (VTW) are designed to do this that – *engage* employees throughout the organization.

The 20 Questions of a Successful Valued Touchpoint Workshop

Successful Valued Touchpoint Workshops (VTW) answer 20 sequential questions. These 20 questions help ensure success and produce the needed output.

1. What experience are we improving?

2. Who needs to be involved? Establishing the team.

3. What is our Workshop Schedule?

4. What is the first meeting agenda?

5. What is the Workshop Charter?

6. Who takes which role?

7. How/when are we going to gain approvals?

8. What is the map of the current state?

9. Do we have the right scope? Mapping the current state can change the scope as outlined in the Charter.

10. What can we benchmark and learn – how is the current state performing for both external and internal customers – what is the value to the customer of each touchpoint?

11. What additional information do we need – what don't we know that we need to know?

12. What foundations do we need to apply/develop? Sometimes the Touchpoint Team needs to establish working foundations, such as an Identity, to do its best work

13. What would the experience be if we could start with a blank canvas and without limitations? Break out of the proverbial box and think big – great ideas can come from this exercise.

14. What is the map of our desired state?

15. How do we make each touchpoint in the desired state a Valued Touchpoint? Ask and answer each of the four Valued Touchpoint Questions.

16. What is our implementation plan and how do we execute it?

17. What is our communication plan and how do we execute it?

18. How do we measure the desired state?

19. How do we sustain and continuously improve the desired state?

20. What are the results? Measure and report.

Rule: If a current state does not exist – if the Team is designing a new experience – skip questions 8, 9, and 10.

187

Valued Touchpoint Workshop output and flow

Answering these questions produces the Workshop output – Valued Touchpoints. It is that simple. The primary steps will look like this:

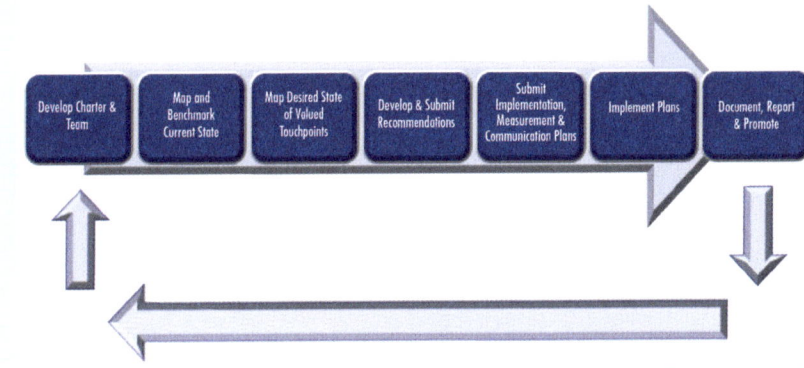

| Develop Charter & Team | Map and Benchmark Current State | Map Desired State of Valued Touchpoints | Develop & Submit Recommendations | Submit Implementation, Measurement & Communication Plans | Implement Plans | Document, Report & Promote |

Developing a Touchpoint Team to map current and desired touchpoints

Each Valued Touchpoint Workshop (VTW) is comprised of a team of colleagues called a Touchpoint Team. A VTW may be made up of a departmental or cross functional Touchpoint Team. Most Teams are cross-functional as it is rare that a customer experience is impacted only by a single department.

Touchpoint Teams drive organic improvements

Touchpoint Teams are made up of the employees who develop, assist and deliver customer touchpoints. In other words, customer-engaging employees and those

> **Touchpoint Team**
> The team of relevant individuals that make up the participants of a Valued Touchpoint Workshop.

who support them. As a result, Valued Touchpoint Workshops are an organic, holistic and bottom-up method for building customer-centricity.

Each Touchpoint Team is ideally made up of about 5 – 7 members, although typically the Team is much larger. Permanent Team members are individuals who represent the touchpoints in the experience or journey being mapped. In addition to permanent members, the Team may need specific expertise at periodic times. For instance, the Team may need someone to report to them on relevant market research or help them design a questionnaire to use in surveying relevant colleagues and customers. This is an example of a support or ad hoc team member.

There are four roles within the Team: Facilitator, Producers, Customer and Support

- **Facilitator.** Guides the group to produce the output. The facilitator role is crucial and is best filled by someone not directly responsible for developing or delivering the touchpoints in question. This individual may be an outside facilitator, a member of the organization's quality function if one exists (e.g. Six Sigma), or someone else who can shepherd the Team on an ongoing basis. The facilitator also captures the group's output. The facilitator is the most important role in the Team's success. Facilitator training is critical (see the TOUCHPOiNT POWER Toolbox for facilitator training).

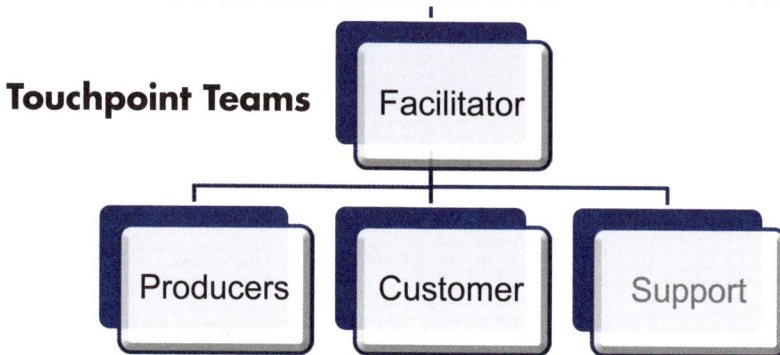

Touchpoint Teams

```
                    ┌──────────────┐
                    │  Facilitator │
                    └──────┬───────┘
         ┌─────────────────┼─────────────────┐
   ┌───────────┐    ┌───────────┐     ┌───────────┐
   │ Producers │    │  Customer │     │  Support  │
   └───────────┘    └───────────┘     └───────────┘
```

- **Producers.** The group of employees who will produce the Workshop's output.

- **Customer.** Of course the best-case scenario is that actual customers are involved in the process. In lieu of actual customers or when actual customers can't attend, the role of customer will need to be played by an employee. If this is the case, then this role is best filled by an employee who is close to customers. This role plays a key dynamic in helping the Team create truly customer-centric Valued Touchpoints. Whoever plays the "customer" should stay in character and function solely to provide the Team with a customer's perspective. To do so, it is best if this role is mostly passive. In other words and for the most part, the "customer" should withhold input until asked questions by the Producers. Producers should get in the habit of asking the customer questions.

Note: It is important that members of the Touchpoint Team feel comfortable to freely express opinions. If a supervisory or management person is a part of the Touchpoint Team, it is typically best for them

189

to play the "customer" as long as they have a recent history of customer knowledge/contact and the others respect this person's customer knowledge. Having someone from a higher level in the organization serve as a producer can "quiet" the other producers. This dynamic depends on the culture of the company and the leadership style of individuals involved.

- **Support.** Support or ad hoc members are colleagues or vendors brought in by the Team to add specific intelligence or to perform a specific function – for instance, to conduct a survey.

Conflict will create better results

A key to the quality of the output is the natural conflict between what the customer wants and what the organization can and should practically provide and the related cost. This is why a customer or an employee playing the role of the customer is so valuable. The conflict inherent between these roles on the Team will help the group produce the best Valued Touchpoints.

A standardized desired state

In defining the desired state, the Touchpoint Team recommends standards and best practices for each and every desired state touchpoint. It is this granularity at the touchpoint level that establishes a Valued Touchpoint.

Extending standards to all customer touchpoints

The first attribute of a Valued Touchpoint is that it is "standardized." Standards already exist in your organization. We have already discussed that most calls to a central business phone are answered in a standardized manner. Through VTWs we extend the concept of standardizing to other touchpoints, and eventually, to *all* touchpoints.

Touchpoint Standard: The minimum level of performance for a Valued Touchpoint.

In addition to standardizing touchpoints, VTW's Touchpoint Teams capture and codify touchpoint best practices.

Mine your best practices, an unrealized asset

Best practices happen every day at touchpoints in your organization. You have colleagues who have developed ways or phrases that are especially customer-centric and that work really well. If these best practices are not shared with others who can use them, they are an unrealized asset. One purpose of the

Workshops is to capture these best practices and to share them with those who can apply them when the time, opportunity, or customer allow or suggest.

Touchpoint Best Practice: A defined Valued Touchpoint performance that is above and beyond Standard. Best practices are typically applied if customer, time, or situation suggests or allows. "Defined" best practices are those that have been captured and codified.

Creativity still wanted and needed

While there are probably not to be any deviations from how one answers the phone, many touchpoints do allow for personal interpretations. Establishing standards is not to be seen as an effort to sap the creativity from staff. It is to solve the core problem of inconsistency and provide customers with a consistent experience. We need staff creativity to continually improve touchpoints and to come up with best practices.

Touchpoint Standard

The minimum level of performance for a Valued Touchpoint.

Touchpoint Best Practice

A defined Valued Touchpoint performance that is above and beyond Standard. Best practices are typically applied if customer, time, or situation suggests or allows. "Defined" best practices are those that have been captured and codified.

Touchpoint standards and best practices can cover any number of areas. A standard can be as simple as the phrase used as a first response to a customer who complains: "Thank you so much for sharing your experience with me, I am so sorry …"

There can be touchpoints where the standard offers no option for deviation or best practice. Examples include how a phone is answered, the application of the organization's mark or logo, the number of tomato slices on a hamburger, or the fact that each promotional package includes the business card of the sales rep. A best practice might be that the rep adds a hand-written personal note to the promotional package.

There can be touchpoint standards that can allow for great latitude. Examples include:

- The amount of money an employee can commit the organization to in the service of an employee – for The Ritz-Carlton, it is up to $2,000

- The standard for how a food server first approaches a table might include four components: A welcome, their name, the day's specials, and

191

a request for the customers' beverage order. How the server executes each of the four components is up to them.

- The standard can set parameters or specify how a touchpoint can be individualized – asking a client if they prefer their bill be delivered via postal mail or email and whether they want to pay by check, credit card or transfer

Best practices represent an area where creativity can really flourish. Best practices for different companies may include:

- Call-center rep calling a customer back with additional information or the resolution, eliminating the need for the customer to call again
- Dry cleaner providing a free bottle of water, adding an unexpected value
- Forgiving a late charge, meeting a customer's desired resolution
- Remembering your name
- Replacing a broken part

Best practices can generate appreciation and positive word-of-mouth

In the above example, Cigna Health Care call center reps have twice called me back after I called with questions. They called me back to provide deeper and more thorough information, eliminating my need to potentially call again.

Third Street Dry Cleaners in Jacksonville Beach provides a free cold bottle of water occasionally or when asked. It gets hot in Florida, and the cool water is appreciated.

When my department store credit card switched from Visa to American Express, I was late with my first payment due to the change. When I called, they happily reversed the late charge.

When I broke the lid to our Crate and Barrel tea pot I found out that the store does not sell just the lid. The Crate and Barrel at Millennium Mall in Orlando, Florida, went above and beyond. They had a lid sent us at no charge directly from the manufacturer rather than making us buy a whole new tea pot.

Kathryn and several employees at Lillies Coffee Shop in Neptune Beach remember my name, making my experiences there much more personal.

The fact that these best practices are being shared via *TOUCHPOiNT POWER* serves these businesses as a positive word-of-mouth touchpoint. However, a reminder that these best practices maximize value only if these businesses are already covering the basics.

Capturing output

As the Valued Touchpoint Workshops are ongoing, it is important to have a solid process for capturing output. The Team will generate maps of touchpoints as well as data for each touchpoint in the desired state map.

Think of your business and the definition of a touchpoint: *Each interaction, physical, communication, human and sensory, with and within your organization.*

How many touchpoints might your organization have? Hundreds? Thousands? For many organizations, it is in the tens of thousands, and for some, even more.

In building the Consistency Competency of standardizing touchpoints, it is important to capture the standards and best practice for each touchpoint. A combination of software tools such as process mapping, Excel, Visio, etc. can

Touchpoint Form
The form for capturing and codifying the details of desired state Valued Touchpoints.

help serve and automate this need. Capturing output in an easy-to-access tool helps ensure the ongoing benefit of the work.

As experiences are mapped it is important to distinguish one touchpoint from another. And as the practice of mapping current and desired states expands, there is value in being able to find, sort, and/or categorize touchpoints.

> Note: You will find Brigman's Touchpoint Naming Convention™, in the Resources Section in the back of the book and it (Doc # 021, Brigman's Touchpoint Naming Convention) can be downloaded at www.touchpointpower.com/resources.

Secret: Large organizations need to use a naming convention for touchpoints when mapping the current and especially the desired state.

Open-source Customer Experience Management

I call this organic approach to building customer-centricity "open-source CEM." Through this process of Valued Touchpoint Workshops (VTW) frontline employees get to design and implement the Valued Touchpoints they deliver. They improve the processes and touchpoints to better meet both customer and internal needs. This somewhat mirrors open source software where the user can take the foundational software code and improve it to better meet needs.

This type of organic method drives significant benefits that probably contributed to the results of Professor Nutt's study of implementation strategies. In my

193

experience, customer-engaging staff will be far more willing to embrace standards and best practices developed by their peers then those dictated to them from above.

Remember Sarah who returned calls in two hours and her colleague Samuel who returned calls in two days? Imagine the difference to Sarah, Samuel and their colleagues if a team of their peers determines that the standard for returning all calls is to be four hours, versus their supervisors or executives making that same decision and announcing it as an edict?

Open-Source CEM
The process of frontline employees designing and implementing the Valued Touchpoints they deliver.

Truth: There is greater buy-in for the established touchpoint standard and a deeper commitment to its implementation if those who are called on to deliver it are the ones who establish the Valued Touchpoint standard.

Benefiting the organization, employees and customers

The power of open-source CEM to the organization is the scale and speed with which Valued Touchpoints can be implemented and the benefits realized – improving both customer experiences and internal efficiencies, and the organization's bottom line.

The power of open-source CEM to employees is the empowerment it instills along with the opportunity to improve their professional quality of life. They get to improve their internal touchpoints and processes along with improving customer touchpoints.

The power of open-source to customers is the relevance of the resultant Valued Touchpoints to what they are wanting or needing to accomplish along their journey.

Engaging employees has shown to have significant benefits for building customer-centricity. This is supported by Temkin Group research.

Engaged employees are an asset to companies, especially CX leaders

Do something that is good for their company even if it is not expected of them — 84% / 24%

Make a recommendation about an improvement that can be made in their company — 60% / 17%

Engaged employees do more for their companies

Recommend that a friend or relative apply for a job within their company — 56% / 12%

Committed to helping their company succeed — 99% / 17%

Try their hardest to do a good job for their company — 95% / 66%

■ Highly engaged employees

Look for a new job outside their company during the next six months — 25% / 32%

■ Disengaged employees

Taken two or more days of sick leave in last 30 days — 18% / 25%

Companies with very good customer experience (CX)
25% / 75%

Highly/moderately engaged employees

Less engaged employees

Companies with mediocre and poor CX
30% / 70%

Customer experience leaders have more engaged employees

Base: 2,435 U.S. consumers employed in for-profit organizations
Source: Temkin Group report: *Employee Engagement Benchmark Study*
Copyright © 2012 Temkin Group. All rights reserved.

TEMKIN GROUP
When experience matters

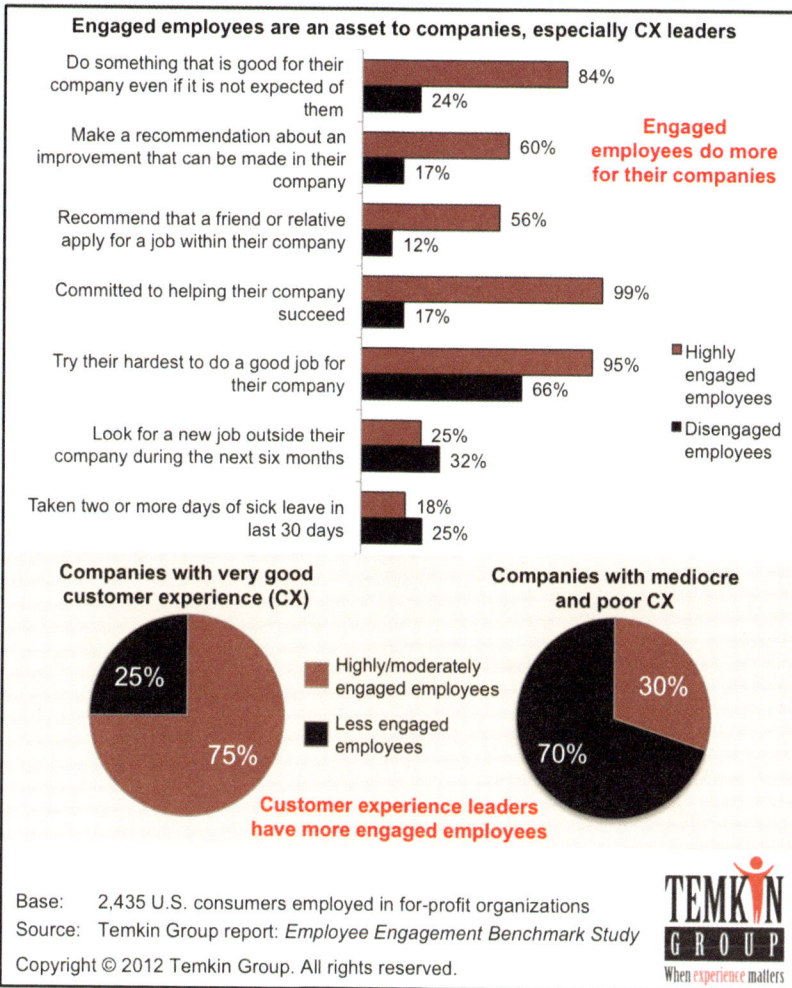

The above research uses the "Temkin Employee Engagement Index," which is based on how much employees agree with three statements:

1. *I understand the overall mission of my company*

2. *My company asks for my feedback and acts upon my input*

3. *My company provides me with the training and the tools that I need to be successful*

Open source CEM through Valued Touchpoint Workshops (VTW) is all about engaging employees in improving touchpoints for both customers and employees in support of the Touchpoint Principle.

195

Note: The following is how GIFT handled a couple of the important questions from the 20 VTW questions they applied to their onboarding new customers pilot. The *TOUCHPOiNT POWER* Toolbox covers each of the 20 questions in detail.

Operationalize/Consistency/VTW/Workshop Schedule
Q3: What is our Workshop schedule?

Paul understood that there were three options in scheduling a Valued Touchpoint Workshop (VTW):

- **Intense.** Five days to try to get it all done. Upside is that this schedule gets the most done in the shortest amount of time. The downside is that all work is rarely accomplished in five days and this schedule doesn't allow for ad hoc work or research that may improve results. Additionally, staff return to their "regular" job way behind. It is like returning from a week vacation without the vacation.

- **Deliberate.** Meet periodically (i.e. weekly) until complete. The upside is that the work can fit comfortably within the schedule of those involved and this schedule allows for work and deliberation between meetings. A down side is that it can take quite a while for the work to be completed and to realize the resultant positive impact.

- **Jump Start.** In this hybrid, the team meets for two to four solid days and periodically thereafter until complete.

Paul chose the Jump Start approach for the onboarding new enterprise customer pilot and sent out invitations to each of the ten Touchpoint Team members for a three-day launch to be followed by weekly 90-minute meetings. He set the periodic meetings to span ten weeks knowing that he could add additional meetings if needed.

Operationalize/Consistency/VTW/Roles
Q5: Who takes which role?

Todd, the senior person on the Touchpoint Team, was a natural to assume the role of the customer when there wasn't an actual customer involved. Todd had been a call center rep before transitioning to training as an onsite Enterprise trainer. Todd was now a training supervisor. The final roles were Otto as facilitator, Todd as the customer, and all of the rest as producers.

Touchpoint Teams

Facilitator

Producers   Customer   Support

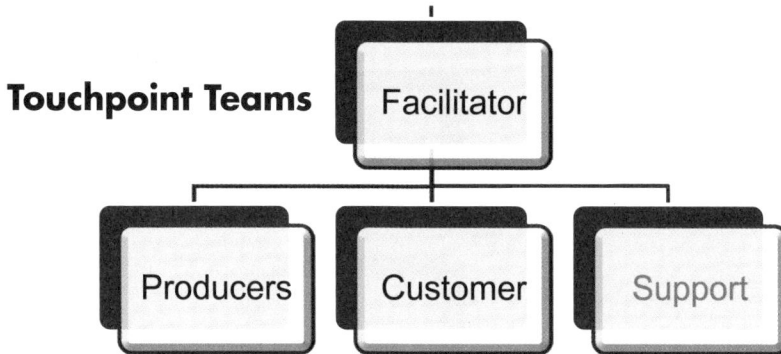

Truth: Nothing will get a group to better understand and own customer needs and points of view than an actual customer.

Secret: Try to get an actual customer to attend at least one day of the VTW (preferably when you are determining value – VTW question #10). If an actual customer can't participate, be sure to have a strong customer "role" on the team. If a customer does attend, take a picture of them. Then post it for every Team meeting where there isn't a customer present. The picture will serve as an ongoing reminder of the valid points the customer made and the need to meet their needs.

Operationalize/Consistency /VTW/Governance
Q 7. How/when are we going to gain approvals?
Paul knew that Governance is one key to maximizing the utility and benefits of VTWs. The Workshops need an oversight layer with a broad view to ensure continuity between different Workshops, in addition to a process for decisions on Team recommendations. Paul, Otto and the Customer Council set it up so that Workshop recommendations would flow to the Council for evaluation and a structured response:

- Accepted w/o conditions/changes
- Accepted with conditions/changes
- Require additional information
- Rejected with explanation

197

Their Valued Touchpoint Workshop hierarchy looked like this:

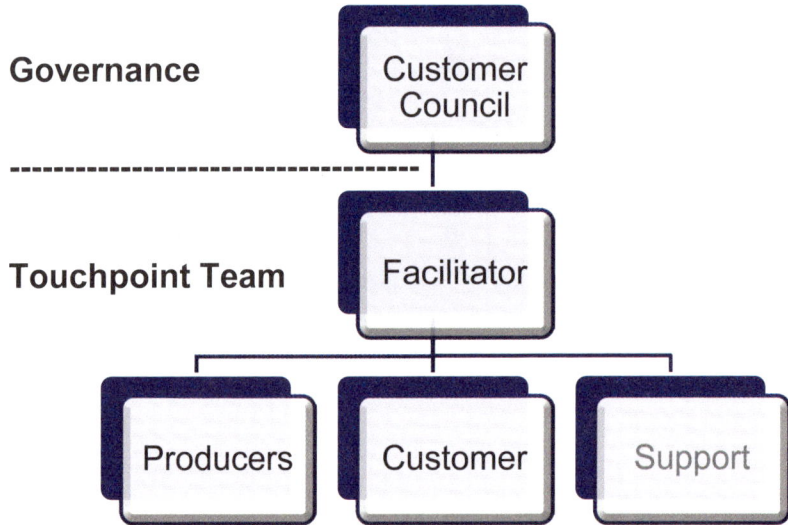

The Customer Council will send their response back to the Workshop to address. Once a recommendation is accepted, an implementation plan must be developed by the Touchpoint Team. While Paul and Otto knew that implementation can be done on a touchpoint basis, they decided it would be best for their implementation plan to be developed for the entire onboarding desired state rather than on a touchpoint by touchpoint basis.

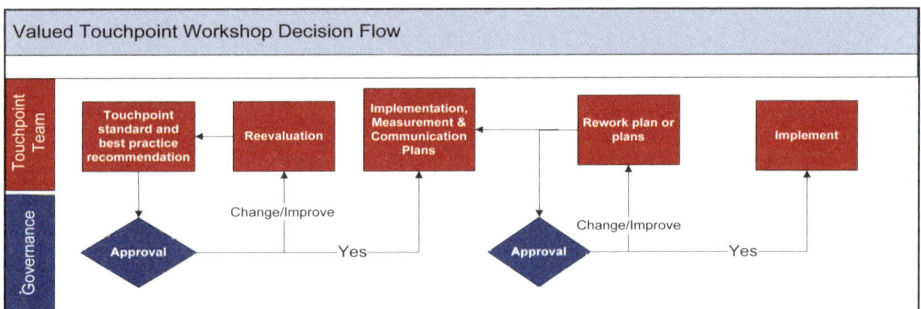

Operationalize/Consistency/VTW/Valued Touchpoints

Q 15 How do we make each touchpoint in the desired state a Valued Touchpoint?

For each touchpoint, internal and external, the team will ask the Four Valued Touchpoint Questions:

1. **Customer.** What is the customer trying to accomplish – what do they need, want or value at this touchpoint?

2. **Identity.** How can we best meet customer needs and wants – make it easier for them – while advancing (or not detracting from) our Values, Identity and Experience Strategy? How do we want our customer to feel?

3. **Touchpoint.** What are our goals with this touchpoint and how can we accomplish them?

4. **Best practice.** What current and/or potential best practice would "wow" the customer?

Note: While it is best to ask the Customer and Identity questions (1 and 2) at each touchpoint, these can be asked at the experience level rather than at each touchpoint.

Secret: Post these questions for each and every subsequent Workshop meeting along with the simple Valued Touchpoint hierarchy of standardization lenses – customer, Identity, touchpoint, and best practices.

Otto took the Producers through the four questions for each of the desired state touchpoints, turning inconsistent touchpoints into Valued Touchpoints.

Deep Dive: "Flirting" with Customers

While in Helsinki, Finland speaking at a conference, I met Mervi Metsanen-Kalliovaara, an owner of a series of lingerie stores (www.patricia.fi). She provided a great example of how an in-depth examination of an important touchpoint to improve customer engagement can lead to dramatic business improvement.

In examining the typical retail sales experience, Mervi found the, "May I help you" (or similar in Finnish) opening line of most sales associates inadequate and one that actually inhibited customer engagement. Mervi wanted to develop a better initial human touchpoint – a way for her associates to engage with customers in order to increase customer and employee satisfaction and business success.

Mervi developed a training process to improve those important opening touchpoints of her customers' retail sales experience. Being a lingerie store, she naturally called it "flirting" with customers.

199

The idea was to get away from the typical yes/no question of "May I help you" and to actually engage with the customer. The training was built around engaging the customer in a real conversation. The opening by the associate was to focus on complimenting something the customer was wearing (as long as the compliment was sincere), or discussing the weather or any other relevant topic that would open up the probably of an actual conversation.

The increase in sales per transaction and overall revenue was dramatic across Mervi's stores. She started to track the sales of individual sales associates and found that those better at engaging had better sales per customer.

For Mervi, examining and transforming key touchpoints of her customers' retail experience into Valued Touchpoints improved customer engagement and business results.

How can your employees improve their touchpoints to better engage with customers?

Deep Dive: A Boisterous Welcome

The Moe's Southwest Grill® restaurant is the: *Home of the popular "Welcome to Moe's®!" greeting and pop-culture inspired menu and atmosphere. Moe's Southwest Grill is a fun and engaging fast-casual concept serving a wide variety of fresh, made-to-order Southwest fare.*

Each time a new customers walks in the door they hear a chorus from the employees, "Welcome to Moe's."

Here is how the minds at Moe's Southwest Grill explain it: "The first thing you'll hear when you walk into the restaurant is an enthusiastic "Welcome to Moe's!" It's more than a greeting; it's a way of life for the folks who customize each meal fresh to order right in front of the guest."

This "enthusiastic" welcome is a key touchpoint in the brand's efforts to build its Identity and the probability of greater customer engagement and success.

Intelligence an important aspect of Workshops and the 20 questions

Paul, Otto and Lucy all knew that a key to turning intelligence into action is the cycle of incorporating customer feedback into the ongoing efforts of Valued Touchpoint Workshops. Customer and internal Intelligence can support changes needed to develop and/or deliver a

Valued Touchpoint. Intelligence can also point to where a new touch-point is needed to best meet customer needs and wants.

Rule: For a Touchpoint Team to develop and deploy the most effective Valued Touchpoints, it needs timely, relevant and accurate transactional and voice of the customer (VOC) data.

There are three questions focused on intelligence:

Q: 10. What can we benchmark and learn – how is the current state performing for both external and internal customers – what is the value?

Q: 18. How do we measure the desired state?

Q: 20. What are the results? Measure and report.

Lucy was integrally involved in helping the Team benchmark the current state, determine how to measure the desired state, and report results for the onboarding pilot.

Rant: The Challenge to CEM if Finance is your "Power Core"

In her 2006 book, *Chief Customer Officer: Getting Past Lip Service to Passion-ate Action©* (Jeanne Bliss, Publisher Jossey-Bass 2006), Jeanne Bliss introduces the concept of an organization's "power core." Bliss believes it is important to understand which department in your company wields the greatest power.

In my experience, organizations with Finance as their Power Core will be Customer Experience challenged. It is not that Finance isn't purposefully cus-tomer-centric; it is just that they often find it hard to quantify its benefit.

Easy to quantify expenses

The expense side of the ledger is typically black and white – it is clear what the impact will be. Here is where Finance tempts chief executives. Chief executives are charged with hitting numbers. It is not uncommon that Finance can deliver short-term dollars by cutting out or reducing aspects of customer service.

Remember our example about shipping? "If we go from 2–day to 5–day shipping for the rest of the year we can save $19 million dollars." Executives charged with delivering their numbers "no matter what" are often tempted by the devil that is short term gain.

The savings temptation may also include longer-term decisions. The classic example is offshoring American call centers to foreign countries. Finance was

able to sell this idea based on the expense side saving of 30% on call center costs. Jobs for America reports that in the 1980s and 1990s 600,000 American call center jobs were sent off shore. A challenge is that rarely do decisions involving customers impact just a single side of the ledger.

Did most organizations that off-shored their call centers save 30%? Absolutely. The resulting problem showed up on the revenue side of the ledger. Expenses shrunk, but for some, so did revenues. Customers engaging with call center reps with thick accents who could only respond to an issue by reading a standard response from a script did not create a positive customer touchpoint. These types of touchpoints are an important reflection of the organization. They often impact both Customer Relationship and Transactional Journeys.

ROI includes revenue

Customers complained and some defected from organizations that sent call centers to other countries. While expenses went down, for some, so did revenue. The actual return on investment (ROI) was negative for some organizations that transferred call centers offshore.

Going back to the original decision, while Finance could dot the i's and cross the t's on the expenses that could be saved taking the call center off shore, the impact on revenue was a grey area. Impact on revenue couldn't be accurately quantified or was ignored.

This inability to easily quantify the impact of service reductions on revenue is an ongoing problem that lends itself to poor short-term decisions that, over time, erode the effectiveness of customer touchpoints, experiences and journeys. This is one primary reason for correlating customer experience metrics to financial metrics such as revenue. This provides the customer experience argument with relevant data.

Secret: Don't bring opinions to a data fight.

Which department is your Power Core?

Understand which department in your organization holds the most power over most executive decisions.

Truth: Most organizations with Finance as its power core are not typically customer-centric and will have trouble becoming customer-centric *without correlating customer experience and financial metrics, or changing the power core.*

Speak in terms they understand

Whether Finance is your power core or not, they have a seat at the executive table. And as a result, you need to work hard to get CEM into their language.

The language of senior executives – the primary language they understand – is financial. That is their world. When a macro metric like Net Promoter score or customer satisfaction goes from 27 to 31, senior executives typically have one question, so what? How does that impact our financials?

I have seen companies with the best customer experience intentions – where senior executives say all of the right things – however, CEM quickly turns into a passing fad. Why? Because the organization couldn't put customer experience in the language of their senior executives – financial.

Secret, Truth, and Rule; Quickly correlate your customer experience metrics with financial metrics.

A huge success

Otto's onboarding Valued Touchpoint Workshop was a huge success and laid a solid foundation for his additional Workshop pilots.

Operationalize/Consistency/VTW/Case Study
Onboarding pilot establishes early win and Consistency Competency

Case Study: The following is a case study of an actual VTW pilot of onboarding new customers.

Deep Dive: A VTW Case Study of Onboarding New Clients

Situation

The market-leading global manufacturer my team worked with was a product innovator. However, as its market matured, it was realizing a diminishing return on innovation as its differentiator. As a result, it sought to enhance growth through customer experience as a differentiator.

This company not only held the largest market share, but also enjoyed an overall Net Promoter score significantly higher than its primary competitors.

Plan

A key part of the CEM Plan was to launch a pilot Valued Touchpoint Workshop to improve the customer-centricity of onboarding new reseller accounts.

203

Benchmark. Net Promoter Score; Overall

How likely are you to recommend...

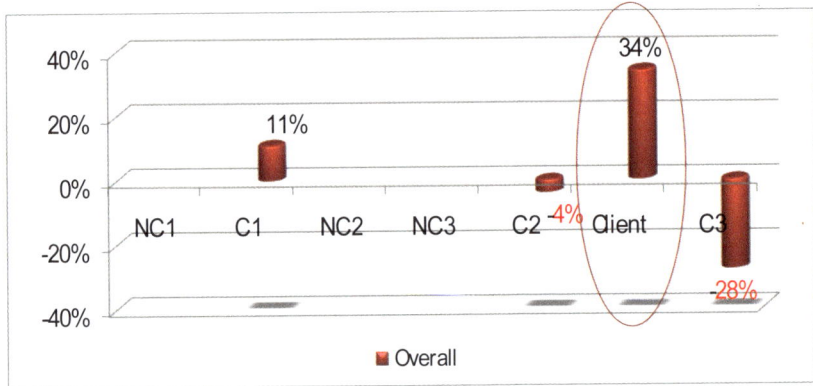

NC = Non-Competitor serving customer, C = Direct Competitor

Its resellers sold directly to the consumer. The pilot Workshop's goals were to improve this important experience while demonstrating the organization's ability to build the Consistency Competency, become more customer-centric, and quantify resultant improvements in financial metrics.

A cross functional Touchpoint Team was assembled to answer the 20 Valued Touchpoint Workshop questions. The Touchpoint Team established both practical and emotional goals for the desired state.

Practical goals

- Provide
    - Information (set expectations)
    - Tools for success
- Have the process be
    - Quick
    - Easy
    - Logical
    - Consistent
- Shorten time for reseller to get up and selling product

Emotional goals

- Wow new customers
- Foster partnership

- Have customers feel appreciated
- Engender loyalty

Benchmark

An early task was to benchmark "likelihood to recommend" (Net Promoter score) of onboarded new resellers across:

- This client
- Direct competitors
- Non-competitors (non-competitive manufacturers of other products that also serve the new reseller account)

Primary Research

Experiments, investigations, or tests carried out to acquire data first-hand, rather than being gathered from published sources.

Source: businessdictionary.com

The results from primary research by an independent research firm were shocking – this market leading company had a Net Promoter score (NPS) *with new resellers* that trailed all but one of its primary competitors. Additionally, its NPS significantly trailed other resellers serving these new resellers.

Benchmark. Net Promoter Score; New Accounts

How likely are you to recommend…

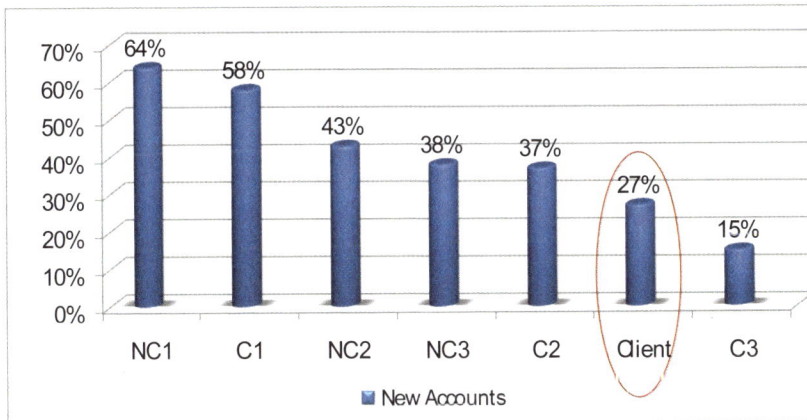

NC = Non-Competitor, C = Competitor

Financial upside identified

Based on this client's historic NPS data and the Brigman's CX Correlation Formula (see Resources Section or Doc # 500, Brigman's CX Correlation Formula™ at *www.TouchpointPower.com/members)*, we knew the average annual spend

205

for each account across the Net Promoter score segments of Promoters, Passives and Detractors.

Given the average number of new resellers onboarded each year, we were able to quantify the difference if all of the new resellers were Promoters versus Detractors. The difference was $36,000,000 per year. The difference in Lifetime Customer Value was over $1 billion dollars.

Annual spend of all Promoters vs. all Detractors

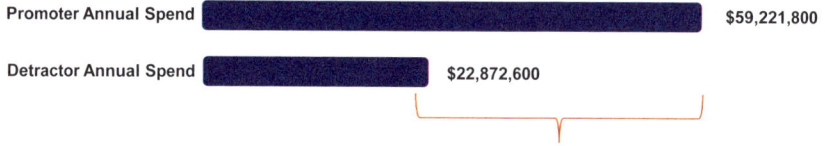

Promoter Annual Spend	$59,221,800
Detractor Annual Spend	$22,872,600

All Promoters vs. all Detractors
- **$36,000,000 per year difference/upside**
- **Over $1 Billion per year difference in lifetime customer value**

While all of the new resellers probably couldn't or wouldn't be Promoters, this calculation established that there were *up to* $36,000,000 on the table annually.

Secret: Really BIG numbers get executives' attention – the bigger, the greater their attention. When possible, express customer experience opportunities or impact in the largest numbers possible. This helps position the strategic importance of customer-centricity.

The current state

The Team inventoried and mapped the current state touchpoints.

- There were 30 touchpoints covering eight different groups or departments
- The field sales reps responsibilities for the onboarding process were onerous and often slowed the approval process
- There were distinct differences in the responsibilities assumed by individual field sales reps verses internal teams
- The reseller had to qualify for a couple of thousand dollars in credit in order to be approved. While there were very few defaults, the approval process was onerous and time consuming. It took an average of 51 days to get a reseller approved and selling product.

- The products and its storage and display unit actually arrived to the reseller separately, requiring the reseller to assemble and stock the display. This, unless the sales rep was available and willing to do so.

- It was uncovered that two internal teams were performing redundant work – one four-person team repeating work already performed by another team

The desired state

A desired state of Valued Touchpoints was defined, mapped, and implemented based on the four Valued Touchpoint Questions. As a result, the organization improved:

- Customer and employee touchpoints
    - Display and product arrived together and assembled
    - Different "Welcome Packages" were personalized for each of the various functions of the reseller's business. This provided relevant information, promotional material and contact information specific to the responsibility of the targeted function.
    - Application process was simplified and streamlined
    - A single person internally was established as the onboarding point of contact and coordinator – improving accessibility and customer communication and eliminating the confusion over whether the new account process would be managed internally or by the sales rep

- Internal efficiencies
    - A four-person team eliminated 28 hours per month in redundant work
    - Shortened time to get new account applications approved and the account selling product from 51 to 12 days
    - The new internal single point of contact improved organizational consistency of the process and relieved the sales rep of significant administrative duties related to new accounts. This enabled sales reps to maintain their focus on their primary responsibility of sales, while improving consistency and responsiveness to the needs of new resellers.

Financial results

On the transition from inconsistent to Valued Touchpoints and an investment of $5,000 to improve touchpoints, the organization:

207

- Shortened time to market for resellers from 51 to 12 days. This added 39 days of product sales per new reseller, adding $7,000,000 annually to the organization's top-line. This also aided resellers desire to sell products sooner, improving their revenue and profit.

Shorten new account days to market

Current State	51 days
Desired State	12 days

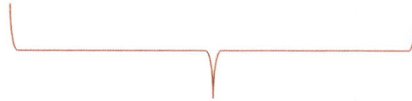

39 extra days of sales = $7,000,000 per year to client

= up to $11,548 to reseller

- Saved a four-person team 28 hours a month in redundant work, $16,800 annually

Amazing ROI

- Investment $5,000   Pre-assembling product kits, welcome letters
- Return annually
  - Additional sales $7,000,000   Shortening time to onboard
  - 28 hours $ 16,800   Eliminating redundancies

                 $7,016,800   =   Return of 1,404 TIMES investment

Note: Return does NOT include any portion of the potential Promoter vs. Detractor upside

Promoter Annual Spend	$59,000,000
Detractor Annual Spend	$23,000,000

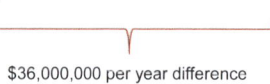

$36,000,000 per year difference

While these results are real, they certainly may not be typical. However, the results do point to the power of a successful Touchpoint Structure that facilitates getting to the granularity of asking and answering the Four Valued Touchpoint Questions, and implementing the results.

Successful pilots lead to dramatic increase in VTWs

With the four pilots complete and success documented, Paul and his group reported results and plans to the EC. Paul proposed a schedule of VTWs and the process for adding facilitators from Customer Service to accommodate the scope of the schedule. The Executive Council (EC) congratulated Paul and his team on the results and approved the schedule for additional Valued Touchpoint Workshops (VTW).

Operationalize/Magic
Magic happening as the Three Competencies converge

Eighteen months in, GIFT was now at a point where it had built its competencies of Identity, Intelligence and Consistency such that they converged. Their Identity Pyramid was complete and implemented, and they had a great start on getting the right information to the right people at the right time. The Workshops continued to be a resounding success. They were incorporating both Identity and Intelligence in improving both customer touchpoints and internal efficiencies. As a result, the bottom line was improving as evident through both macro and financial metrics.

A repeated Customer-Centricity Audit revealed results covered in green, with a few items yellow, and none solid red.

Maggie was pleased that GIFT's overall NPS had increased 15 points, translating into $22.5 million in additional revenue. She was also ecstatic with the significant improvement in NTS (Net Teamwork score) and the corresponding change in attitude around GIFT. There appeared to be a lighter and happier atmosphere in the building with the improved teamwork. Maggie noticed that staff retention was up and GIFT was also attracting better job candidates.

GIFT was realizing the Touchpoint Structure Value Chain that results from the Touchpoint Principle: *The ability to get and keep desired customers and employees is enhanced by consistently delivering Valued Touchpoints.*

Expanding CEM efforts

GIFT expanded the scope of the Valued Touchpoint Workshop program globally and was now applying Workshops to their other lines of business. Otto now had a team of 12 facilitators reporting to him. He was traveling the world, and yes, he really really liked this job.

Benefiting the organization and individuals

Lucy received a nice bonus and took a leave of absence to follow the European tour of a band no one had heard of.

209

Paul now held the position of Chief Customer Officer and sat on the Executive Council.

Boris, Chief Financial Officer, left to join another company where he was advocating that they undertake a strategy to improve customer-centricity as a way to improve financial performance.

Maggie was constantly fielding calls from headhunters offering attractive opportunities to lead significant Silicon Valley software companies. Happy, she didn't return any of the calls.

Operationalize/Summary

Operationalizing a CEM Plan is an exercise in working to build three competencies – Identity, Intelligence and Consistency – in the service of an Experience Strategy.

Key points

- It is important to establish your macro relationship metric and to correlate it to a financial metric such as revenue

- The Implementation Model is summarized in the Touchpoint Principle: *The ability to get and keep desired customers and employees is enhanced by consistently delivering Valued Touchpoints*

- A task of the CEM Plan is to turn inconsistent touchpoints into Valued Touchpoints: *Standardized interaction that is customer-centric while advancing the organization's Values, Identity and Strategy, and the touchpoint's goal(s)*

- Developing and deploying Valued Touchpoints creates a Touchpoint Structure Value Chain

- Valued Touchpoint Workshops (VTW) is the Touchpoint Structure for building the Consistency Competency and the primary vehicle for operationalizing the Identity and Intelligence Competencies – turning inconsistent touchpoints into Valued Touchpoints

- The primary output of VTWs are touchpoint standards, best practices and implementation, measurement and communication plans

- In larger organizations, VTW output goes to a governance layer for evaluation and approval

- The Measure step feeds the other three steps of the Touchpoint Structure Implementation Model

- Voice of Customer (VOC) research may need to start VOIC (Voice of Internal Customer)

- Net Teamwork score is a macro VOIC metric based on internal cooperation

- In addition to the macro relationship metric, it is important to set up listening posts:
  - Along the customer journey to measure performance, drivers of the macro metric, and Identity
  - Internally at the conclusion of specific customer experiences to measure internal systems and process and the performance of individual teammates

- Consider a Customer Council as a means of engaging the organization in the holistic customer journey, solving customer and internal issues, developing CX dashboards and as the governance level of Valued Touchpoint Workshops

- Consider a Customer Room to display customer touchpoints along their journey stages

- Pilot Valued Touchpoint Workshops to demonstrate success and to start to build the Consistency Competency and Touchpoint Structure

- There are 20 questions, that if followed sequentially, will develop the desired output and improve the probability of a successful VTW

- To help create needed conflict and to ensure that the customer's perspective is a part of developing Valued Touchpoints, enlist the involvement of customers, or, have an employee play the role of a customer in VTWs

- Define standards and capture best practices for each Valued Touchpoint in a Touchpoint Form

- Magic happens when Identity and Intelligence intersect in Valued Touchpoint Workshops (VTW)

211

CHAPTER 10:
PUTTING IT
ALL TOGETHER

Where to Start and Secrets to Success

Every journey worth taking starts with a single step.
Unknown

Secrets/Introduction

While this chapter starts to signal the conclusion of the *TOUCHPOINT POWER* book, it is my hope that this is the beginning of your journey to a successful Touchpoint Structure and reaping the many benefits of customer-centricity.

After reading this short Chapter, you will better understand where and how to start or continue your CEM efforts. Insights are provided for how to start big – if you have leadership support and resources – or start smart – if you have to win support.

Tips are shared for large organizations when their Valued Touchpoint Workshops scale beyond two or three.

Secrets/Starting Big
Following the model and getting to multiple simultaneous Workshops

Organizations that decide to start big typically aren't doing so as a result of a business case. There is often a change in leadership, or someone important went to a conference or read a book or talked with a peer, and becoming customer-centric is now the next big thing.

All of a sudden the organization is appointing a customer experience leader, building a team and committing resources to differentiating and making a cultural change.

Where and how to start depends on a number of factors. With the right leadership support and resources your organization can successfully start big by working the Touchpoint Structure Implementation Model as designed: Conduct a thorough Assessment, develop the Experience Strategy and CEM Plan, implement the Plan on a grand scale, and measure the results. Just follow the steps as outlined in *TOUCHPOiNT POWER*.

Starting big often is interpreted as starting fact-based rather than speed-based. Warning! I have seen situations where all of the Five Organizational Success Factors (Independence, Support, Resources, Expertise, and Political Acumen) were aligned at the outset and the organization decided to start fact-based, as per the Model. Over time, the lack of early wins due to time devoted to the required due diligence, change in chief executives, or changing market dynamics sapped executive commitment to CEM.

Secret: You can successfully start big if the five organizational success factors are in place and the Four Ss (Scope, Scale, Sequence and Success) have been answered.

Secrets/Starting Smart
It's all about early wins

Of course you don't have to apply *TOUCHPOiNT POWER* on a grand scale. You can use the methodologies and tools just to tackle a specific customer experience challenge/opportunity. Or perhaps you want to just get started to see where it goes and the traction it generates. It could be that you know that Customer Experience Management (CEM) is the right focus for your organization, but leadership isn't there yet. In these cases, you need to start smart.

What's the best first step?

If I had to boil starting smart down to a single first step, I would suggest either starting a Customer Council or a launching a Value Touchpoint Workshop pilot, or both. Either of these can start constructive dialogs internally while also producing meaningful results and early wins.

For the Customer Council, gather who you can – one manager and one customer-facing staff (or the individual in small companies) from as many departments that will participate as possible. Work to get the Council out of their siloed view and to start to see the holistic customer journey. Start to generate understanding of the problem touchpoints customers face, and how they impact the customer, employees and organization. Address the low-hanging fruit the Council can easily improve. This will enhance both customer and employee experiences. Share metrics and land a customer experience dashboard.

For a Workshop, choose a potentially impactful experience, assemble a relevant team and ask and answer as many of the 20 Valued Touchpoint Workshop Questions as possible.

It doesn't really take much to launch either the Council or a Workshop. Take what you can from *TOUCHPOiNT POWER* and apply it while working hard to quantify the results. Build wins and the ability to quantify. Eventually leadership should come around to the value of Customer Experience Management (CEM).

Secret (and strong advice): Whether starting smart or big, when at all possible, start speed-based and quickly demonstrate results.

Small companies keep it simple

As previously mentioned, *TOUCHPOINT POWER* was written for the enterprise level perspective. In comparison, small companies typically enjoy a simpler customer journey and are made up of small teams or individual employees versus large departments. Small companies need to take the concepts and ideas presented and scale them down to meet their needs – keep it simple.

Just as in a large company, start with a workshop and/or your version of a Customer Council. Your Customer Council might include all or most employees. Regardless of size, schedule periodic meetings to discuss what employees are observing and hearing from customers, and what can be done to improve and track customer experiences and internal efficiencies.

For your version of a Valued Touchpoint Workshop, you probably won't need to answer all 20 questions – just those that make sense for you and your small business. Commit to mapping your customers' journeys and turning your inconsistent touchpoints into Valued Touchpoints.

Secret: Small business owners and leaders need to recognize that your workshop output needs to be driven by staff to maximize success. Early on, resist the temptation to drive the conversation and answer all of the questions. This will only quiet staff and make this your initiative instead of theirs. Your best role is actually the customer so that suggestions and recommendations surface primarily from your staff.

Define Identity, gain Intelligence and standardize touchpoints

Building the Three Customer-Centricity Competencies is just as important for small businesses as it is for large. In fact, building the competencies should help a small business become larger and more successful. And because there typically isn't the political and matrixed nature of large organizations, building the competencies can be easier.

Answer the Identity Pyramid questions and survey customers. It's not hard to survey – use paper surveys, use an online tool like SurveyMonkey - just gather relevant intelligence. Then bring the Identity and survey results into your version of a Valued Touchpoint Workshop.

Positive word of mouth, touchpoint by touchpoint

Word of mouth is so important for small businesses. Designing and delivering Valued Touchpoints will help generate the positive word of mouth that can grow a small business. There may be nothing a small business can do that will positively impact results more than becoming truly customer-centric.

> Note: The TOUCHPOiNT POWER Toolbox is available in several customized versions, including one especially for small businesses. Concepts, forms and tools are appropriately scaled down and simplified to better serve the needs of small business.

However it is that your organization decides to start, the organization will need to approach customer journeys with the same rigor that manufacturers approach their product journey. And whether you start big or smart, there will be both challenges and magic in your Customer Experience Management (CEM) efforts.

Magic happens with employees and at the intersection of the competencies

Magic will happen as front-line employees get excited by the empowerment this open-source CEM process generates. Their excitement will breathe life and results into CEM, generating momentum. Momentum will also build with early wins, and with the ability to quantify success in financial terms.

The greatest magic at the touchpoint level happens when the Three Competencies intersect – when your Identity and the right information to the right people at the right time intersect with the Four Valued Touchpoint Questions. It is magical. It is then that the long-term value of the Touchpoint Structure Value Chain will start to be realized. The results are magical for customers, employees and the organization.

Challenges getting to the needed granularity

Chances are you will encounter challenges – challenges in generating momentum, resources and winning over internal detractors. You will also be challenged in balancing the ongoing efforts across each of the Three Competencies. It can be especially challenging to get down the granularity required to ask and answer the Four Valued Touchpoint Questions, and implement and measure the results. But don't despair. These are common challenges. Keep focused, and remember, the barriers you overcome are the ones that block your competitors from achieving customer-centricity. That is why there are so few customer-centric companies and why your organization's CEM success will create a defendable competitive advantage.

Oversight ensures compatibility

With success, large organizations applying *TOUCHPOiNT POWER* will eventually get to the point where multiple Valued Touchpoint Workshops (VTW) are operating simultaneously. This is when governance by the Customer Council is especially important. This oversight will make sure that the changes being recommended and made in the various workshops are all compatible and in keeping with the Experience Strategy. Additionally, this oversight ensures smooth handoffs. The Customer Council will watch for different workshops working on similar or sequential experiences. It is not uncommon that workshops are combined, postponed, or redirected based on the work of another workshop. This oversight layer in large organizations is also responsible for capturing and sharing workshop best practices.

Secret: For large organizations, it can be highly productive to have the facilitators leading different VTWs meet on an ongoing basis to discuss challenges and best practices. The output of these meetings can be taken to the governance level to drive continuous improvement of the workshop, governance, communication, and implementation processes.

Have a Team member rotation plan

As your Consistency Competency builds, there will be a need to rotate Touchpoint Team members. Part of overall Workshop effectiveness is to have a plan for Team member rotations.

Secret: Don't implement wholesale replacement of a Touchpoint Team. Rotate new Team members in on a staggered schedule to maintain Team knowledge and momentum.

Get to the granularity

Whatever you do, get down to the touchpoint level with your changes. Ask the Four Valued Touchpoint Questions and implement the results. This

Touchpoint Structure Value Chain™

Touchpoint Results	Standardized customer interactions…
Customer Experience Results	create consistently positive customer experiences…
Customer Journey Results	Motivating journey progression…
Strategic Results	generating the desired Identity/perceptual asset…
Purpose Results	maximizing the ability to get and keep customers…
Financial Results	positively impacting the top and bottom lines.

is the ultimate key. This is where it has to happen to maximize benefits and achieve the value chain. This is what your competitors aren't doing.

Whack-a-mole is not the answer

Recognize and get others to recognize that solving a few customer problems is not customer-centricity and will not be the source of dramatic change. Customer-centricity is cultural. Cultural changes require time to work into the actual DNA of the organization. That is one reason it is so challenging and why the benefits are so significant.

Secrets/Ongoing Workshops
Your Touchpoint Structure never stops

Your organization changes touchpoints and develops new ones on an ongoing basis. As such, it is important to continually work to consistently achieve and live your Experience Strategy and Identity. These Valued Touchpoint Workshops don't represent a program or initiative that starts today and ends at some point in the future. Key to customer-centricity is that it is ongoing – that standardizing touchpoints via VTWs is a Competency that becomes a part of your organization's DNA. It is through this Touchpoint Structure that your organization will tactically address the core experience problem and drive the cultural changes that produce a defendable competitive advantage for the long-term.

Rule: While individual VTWs will start and stop, VTWs as a tool of the Consistency Competency never, ever stop.

Secrets/Secrets to Success
Holistic view of the Implementation Model aids efforts

Just as a holistic view of the customer journey aids efforts to improve its components – the experiences and touchpoints along the journey – so too does a holistic view of the Implementation Model aid efforts. It is with this holistic view of the Model that CX leaders can build wins along the primary components of each step of the Model. These incremental wins improve the efficacy of the Model overall.

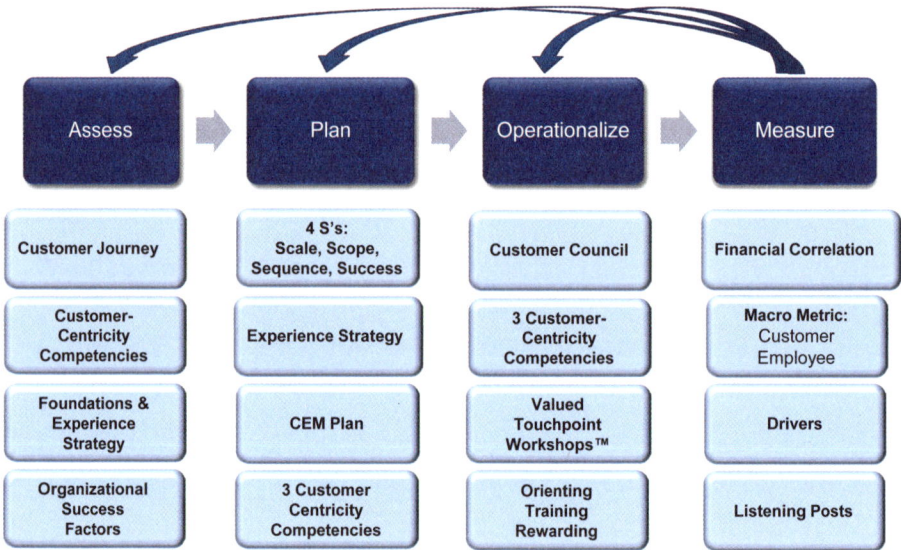

Assess	Plan	Operationalize	Measure
Customer Journey	4 S's: Scale, Scope, Sequence, Success	Customer Council	Financial Correlation
Customer-Centricity Competencies	Experience Strategy	3 Customer-Centricity Competencies	Macro Metric: Customer Employee
Foundations & Experience Strategy	CEM Plan	Valued Touchpoint Workshops™	Drivers
Organizational Success Factors	3 Customer Centricity Competencies	Orienting Training Rewarding	Listening Posts

Don't overlook the importance of your head of HR

Secrets to success are numerous. Many are expected such as leadership support, committed resources, successful team members, etc. Outside of the organization's leader, potentially the two most important people to your success are the heads of Finance and HR.

In the medium to large companies there is a need for the head of Finance to bless your financial correlations and to at least not fight your ongoing efforts.

If a customer-centric culture is your goal, you need HR on board. As the typical owners of hiring, orienting, training, evaluating, promoting and compensating, they are important drivers of the organization's culture and Identity. To gain cultural traction, the HR department or person needs to be integrally involved in CEM. To aid this effort, tie Valued

Touchpoints to job classifications as part of the process of integrating HR into CEM efforts.

> Note: The job classification information can be captured in Touchpoint Forms – see Doc # 020, Touchpoint Form at *www. TouchpointPower.com/resources* for a sample of the form with fields for job classifications and complete instructions. The same Touchpoint Form is available as an interactive form in the *TOUCHPOiNT POWER* Toolbox. Tying touchpoints to jobs is invaluable in training current and new staff.

Secrets/3 Keys
Three keys

If I had to boil it down to three initial keys, they would be:

1. Have both internal political and CEM expertise. If both are not represented in the CEM leader or on the team, use mentors for political acumen or consultants/coaches for CEM expertise.

2. From your chief executive, secure the support (both the talk and the walk) and resources needed to maximize the success of your Experience Strategy and CEM Plan

3. Start with a Workshop that will deliver *quantifiable* financial improvements while at the same time improve the lives of fellow colleagues. Be sure to get to and answer the Four Valued Touchpoint Questions and implement the results.

Secrets/Conclusion
Adapt as needed

As I have stressed a number of times, you will need to adapt the concepts and tools to your specific situation. As you do, please let me know how things are going. I welcome your questions and feedback. One of my greatest aspirations is that *TOUCHPOiNT POWER* inspires additional creative thinking and practices around Customer Experience Management.

I will remind you that the journey to achieving customer-centricity is not easy or fast. As with any challenging journey, there are enormous rewards along the way as you and your organization achieve your goals.

221

With success, you will realize rewards both personally and professionally. One of my greatest sources of satisfaction is improving the professional lives of those with whom I serve. It is gratifying to help resolve internal issues that frustrate employees and hinder their ability to do their best job. Helping employees feel that their employer values both them and their customers is powerful. I hope you and your organization get to taste that satisfaction through CEM.

Any journey worth taking starts with a single step. I hope that you have found this touchpoint a powerful guide for your first or next, and subsequent CEM steps.

Best of luck, and remember:

To your customers, you *are* your touchpoints.

At Your Service,

Differentiate and Build a Competitive Advantage, Touchpoint by Touchpoint™

Customer Experience Management
Strategy, Implementation. Measurement

Speaker, Consultant, Coach, Trainer, Author

Office: + 1 904.466.1805
Personal email: Hank@TouchpointGuru.com
Personal Web: *www.TouchpointGuru.com*

Secrets/Summary
Key Points

- You can improve the probability of success of starting big if the five organizational success factors are in place and the Four Ss are answered

- Starting smart is all about early wins

- Highly advised to start speed-based, whether starting big or smart

- Start with something that creates impact – a Customer Council or pilot Valued Touchpoint Workshop

- Magic happens when Identity and Intelligence intersect in Valued Touchpoint Workshops

- Don't avoid the hard work of getting down to the granularity of asking and answering the Four Valued Touchpoint Questions – this is where *TOUCHPOiNT POWER* is generated

- Valued Touchpoint Workshops should never ever stop – the organization is developing and changing touchpoints on an ongoing basis

- Engage HR in your CEM efforts

- Three keys:

  - Have both internal political and CEM expertise. If both are not represented in the CEM leader or on the team, use mentors for political acumen or consultants/coaches for CEM expertise.

  - From your chief executive, secure the support (both the talk and the walk) and resources needed to maximize the success of your Experience Strategy and CEM Plan

  - Start with a Workshop that will deliver *quantifiable* financial improvements while at the same time improve the lives of fellow colleagues. Be sure to get to and answer the Four Valued Touchpoint Questions and implement the results.

- It is important for employee orientation and training to tie each Valued Touchpoint to the job classifications that develop or deliver the touchpoint

- Adapt as needed

- To your customers, you are your touchpoints

- Reach out to me if I can help

- **Enjoy!**

About the Author

"To your customers, you are your touchpoints"

Hank Brigman is recognized as a pioneer and thought-leader in the exploding discipline of Customer Experience Management (CEM). The first to define "touchpoint" on Wikipedia, Hank is known as the "Touchpoint Guru." His expertise, body of work, and dynamic style position Hank as a sought after speaker on stages worldwide.

Quantifiable Success with Fortune 100 Companies

Hank works with organizations large and small. Prominent clients that have realized *quantifiable* improvements include GE, AT&T, Mentor, Travelers, Novartis, Microsoft, Biomet, and Johnson & Johnson. He is laser focused on generating lasting improvements by helping organizations build the competencies that differentiate and establish a competitive advantage. He also addresses the need to determine ROI and translate customer experience into the language of the boardroom – finance. An asset in these efforts is his original formula for correlating a one point movement in "likelihood to recommend" to revenue.

Advancing Customer-Centricity as an Innovator

As co-founder, President/CEO of an early and award-winning customer experience research consultancy, Hank co-invented a process for mapping touchpoints. This original process for inventorying, mapping, evaluating and improving individual customer touchpoints now forms the foundation for many of today's Customer Experience Management methodologies.

Hank shares his expertise and insights through his *TOUCHPOiNTER* newsletter, posts on his *TouchpointTalk.com* blog, and via Twitter *(@ TouchpointGuru)*.

After graduating from university, Hank enjoyed three years as a professional golfer on the mini tours. He still enjoys golf and has recently taken up surfing.

> **"The most valuable program on service excellence I have attended over my 15 years in the industry."**
>
> *-N. Keong, Head, Customer Management*
> *Centre for Innovation and Enterprise*

Hank Brigman
TOUCHPOiNTGuru ™

Building Customer-Centricity
Touchpoint by Touchpoint

- Member, National Speakers Association
- Rave reviews on four continents
- Consulting clients include five Fortune 100 companies
- Fortune 50 head of customer experience
- Co-inventor mapping touchpoint methodology
- First to define "touchpoint" on Wikipedia
- "Expert Corner" blogger for Salesforce.com's Desk.com blog

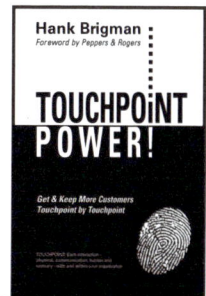

Hank Brigman
Foreword by Peppers & Rogers

TOUCHPOiNT POWER!
Get & Keep More Customers
Touchpoint by Touchpoint

Meeting planner raves

Hank Brigman is a dynamic and engaging speaker. He is a pleasure to work with and the evaluations of his program were outstanding. R. Fortunato, Legal Marketing Association

Dynamic keynotes to improve revenue

Hank Brigman is a passionate and entertaining presenter laser focused on providing attendees with the knowledge and tools to immediately improve business results, touchpoint by touchpoint.

To your customers, you are your touchpoints

Attendees will leave empowered with insights and action items from setting strategy to improving individual customer interactions – or touchpoints.

Hank' practical approach to improving customer experiences is refreshing in its simplicity and ability to help differentiate and build a defendable competitive advantage.

Fresh, current and applicable

As a thought-leader with an active consulting practice, Hank stays on top of emerging trends and best practices. His content is fast-paced and highly relevant to not only surviving, but thriving in today's YouTube and Yelp world.

Attendees will leave empowered with the knowledge, motivation and tools to immediately improve touchpoints and business results for every "customer"

Success for you and your event – book Hank today

+1 904.466.1805   Hank@TouchpointGuru.com   www.TouchpointGuru.com   YouTube

Travels from Jacksonville, Florida

225

Your **TOUCHPOiNT POWER** Toolbox
Comes Loaded with Valuable Training and Tools

The TOUCHPOiNT POWER Toolbox is your comprehensive suite of instructional videos and interactive forms and tools. Based on TOUCH-POiNT POWER, this powerful do-it-yourself (DIY) toolbox guides you and your organization step-by-step through the process of building a customer-centric organization, touchpoint by touchpoint.

I highly recommend Hank's book and more importantly, utilizing his tools to improve your customer experience.

Jack Rawle, Senior Director,
Worldwide Sales Operations & Effectiveness

Your Toolbox can include:

- **Instructional videos** – how to use the toolbox and tips and secrets to improve the success of your customer experience efforts

- A thorough **narrative** of a hypothetical company going through many of the steps, exercises and workshops – learn from their mistakes and successes

- **Mapping training and tools**

  - ☐ Step-by-step mapping instructions – build this competency critical to understanding and improving customer and internal touchpoints

  - ☐ Facilitator training including tools and forms to:

    - ▽ Define the mapping workshop's goals and scope – lay a foundation for success

    - ▽ Run a successful mapping workshop

    - ▽ Customize to meet your needs

▽ Capture mapping results and output – including staff training materials specific to your touchpoints

▽ Allow participants to evaluate the process – input for continuous improvement

- A **formula** that correlates customer experience efforts to revenue

A Toolbox customized for your type of business

Select the version with the narrative and forms geared to your business:

- **Enterprise** – A version with a narrative of an enterprise company and the depth, detail and flexibility to meet the needs of large organizations

- **Small/Medium Business** – A version with a narrative of a small business and instruction, tools and forms scaled to comfortably meet the less complicated needs of small/medium businesses

- **Eye Care Practices** – This Toolbox is customized specifically to improve the patient experience and business results of eye care practices

Check the Toolbox website for more information, to obtain your TOUCH-POiNT POWER Toolbox and to check the availability of additional customized versions.

Save time, effort and resources.

TOUCHPOiNT POWER Toolbox
Do-it-Yourself Customer-Centricity.

www.TouchpointPower.com/Toolbox

227

SECTION IV
RESOURCES

Touchpoint Naming Convention,

Valuable Formula and Availability

of Additional Resources at

www.TouchpointPower.com

Section IV

Resources

Resources/Touchpoint Naming Convention

Brigman's Touchpoint Naming Convention™

This naming convention prescribes the following sequence for naming each touchpoint;

Type.Direction.GeneralDescriptor.SpecificDescriptor

Where:

Type = The type of touchpoint

Direction = The direction of the touchpoint

GeneralDescriptor = A general description of the touchpoint

SpecificDescriptor = A more specific description

Example: An email invitation to a customer dinner to promote the launch of the new super widget might be captured as:

Email.P2C.Invitation.SuperWidgetLaunchDinner

Where

Email = Email is the **type** of touchpoint deployed

P2C = The **direction** of the touchpoint is provider (P) to customer (C). Use whatever abbreviations are relevant for your organization.

Invitation = **General description** of the touchpoint as an invitation

SuperWidgetLaunchDinner = The **specific description** of the invitation

Touchpoint types

Examples of touchpoint types – you will need to add/delete as appropriate for your business

Ad	Form	PR
Article	Gift	Presentation
Blog	Giveaway	Product
Brochure	Human	Proposal
Call	Invoice	Referral
CD	Letter	Store
Collateral	Manual	Survey
Conference	Meeting	Tradeshow
Contract	Newsletter	Training
Demo	Office	Vendor
Dmail (direct mail)	Pkging	Website
Email	PoP (point of purchase)	
Event	Portal	

Direction

It can be highly productive to establish abbreviations to use in the direction component of the naming convention for different departments and entities. Examples include:

S = Sales
M = Marketing
A = Accounting
O = Operations
CS = Customer Service
V = Vendor (can have an abbreviation for each)
P = Partner (can have an abbreviation for each, i.e. F = FedEx)

Descriptors

Use the descriptors as needed but try to be succinct.

In the end, someone reading the name should be able to understand which touchpoint it is by its name. The periods (.) between the components will help sort touchpoints in Excel or various database programs.

As with all tools provided, adapt as needed and let me know how it works for you.

Resources/Financial Correlation
Brigman's CX Correlation Formula™

Correlating 1 point movement in Net Promoter score to top-line revenue

It is easiest to show the formula in an example. Here, we are looking at a very large hypothetical insurance company and the NPS status of their agents. I am using large round numbers in an attempt to make the formula as easy to follow as possible.

Two key concepts:

1. To achieve a change of one NPS percentage point, a total of one percent of your customer universe most change NPS segments (Promoter, Passive, and Detractor)

2. Promoters, Passives and Detractors typically spend/purchase differently, creating an average spend distinction across Promoters, Passives and Detractors

It may take a couple of reads through, but stick with it. This is perhaps one of the most valuable tools in *TOUCHPOiNT POWER*.

Data needed

- NPS percentage for each segment: Promoter, Passives, Detractors

- Total number of customers in customer base

- Annual spend/purchases of an individual customer who responded to the NPS question and their NPS segment (Promoter, Passive, Detractor)

Assumed data points for this example

- NPS survey of agents reveals: 40% Promoters, 50% Passives, 10% Detractors

- Overall NPS = 30% (NPS = % of Promoters – % of Detractors. 40% - 10% = 30%)

- Total agent universe = 500 Agents

- Total agents by NPS classification (agent universe x NPS classification %)

  □ Promoter = 500 Agents x 40% = 200 Agents

  □ Passive = 500 Agents x 50% = 250 Agents

  □ Detractor = 500 Agents x 10% = 50 Agents

233

- Average annual business written by an agent in each NPS classification

  □ Promoter = $10 million

  □ Passive = $5 million

  □ Detractor = $2 million

Revenue

Current revenue = sum of total business for all NPS classifications

Total business for each NPS classification = # Agents by NPS classification x average annual business by NPS classification

```
Promoter = 200 Agents x $10 MM = $2.00   billion
 Passive = 250 Agents x $  5 MM = $1.25   billion
Detractor =  50 Agents x $  2 MM = $  100 million
```
Total: $3.35   billion (Current revenue)

One point movement

A 1 point movement in NPS requires 1% of the agent universe (5 of 500 Agents) to move between NPS segments (Promoter, Passive or Detractors).

To move NPS 1% point up or down:

- 1% (5) of the total universe of 500 Agents has to change classifications
- 1% of Agents (5) has to move between Detractor and Passive OR
- 1% of Agents (5) has to move between Passives to Promoters OR
- Some combination thereof (e.g. 2 Agents from Detractor to Passive and 3 Agents from Passive to Promoter)

Examples of improving 1 NPS % point

New revenue, if all 5 move from detractor to passive,

NPS = 31 (40% promoters, 51% passives, 9% detractors, Promoters – Detractors = NPS)

```
Promoter = 200 Agents x $10 MM = $2.00   billion
 Passive = 255 Agents x $  5 MM = $1.275  billion
Detractor =  45 Agents x $  2 MM = $  90   million
```
Total: $3.365 billion (New revenue)

Gain = new revenue – current revenue
Gain = $3.365 billion - $3.35 B = $15 million

New revenue, if all 5 move from passive to promoter:

NPS = 31 (41% promoters, 49% passives, 10% detractors. Promoters – Detractors = NPS)

Promoter = 205 Agents x $10 MM = $2.05   billion
Passive = 245 Agents x $ 5 MM = $1.225 billion
Detractor =   50 Agents x $ 2 MM = $ 100 million
_____
                                Total: $3.375 billion (New revenue)

Gain = New revenue – Current revenue
Gain = $3.375 billion – 3.35 billion = $25 million

Examples of deteriorating 1 NPS % point

New revenue, if all 5 move from Passive to Detractor,

NPS = 29% (40% promoters, 49% passives, 11% detractors, Promoters – Detractors = NPS)

Promoter = 200 Agents x $10 MM = $2.00   billion
Passive = 245 Agents x $ 5 MM = $1.225 billion
Detractor =   45 Agents x $ 2 MM = $ 90   million
_____
                                Total: $3.315 billion (New revenue)

Loss = new revenue – current revenue
Loss = $3.315 billion - $3.35 B = <$20> million

New revenue, if all 5 move from Promoter to Passive:

NPS = 29 (39% promoters, 51% passives, 10% detractors. Promoters – Detractors = NPS)

Promoter = 195 Agents x $10 MM = $1.950 billion
Passive = 255 Agents x $ 5 MM = $1.275 billion
Detractor =   50 Agents x $ 2 MM = $ 100 million
_____
                                Total: $3.325 billion (New revenue)

Loss = new revenue – current revenue
Loss = $3.325 billion – 3.35 billion = <$25> million

Conclusion

A 1 % point increase or decrease in NPS impacts current revenue between $15 - $25 million

A 1 % point increase or decrease NPS will have an impact on revenue of about $20 MM

235

Resources/Additional Resources
Additional Resources are Available

Visit www.TouchpointGuru.com/Resources or www.TouchpointPower.com/Resources.

These and other documents are freely available - No Login Needed.

Doc #020 Touchpoint Form
A sample form to capture the data for individual Valued Touchpoints.

Doc #021 Brigman's Touchpoint Naming Convention™
As touchpoints are identified and mapped, it is important to name/label each in a program or database – especially relevant for large organizations.

Doc #022 Valued Touchpoint Workshop Process and Decision Flows
The primary flow and decision tree – especially relevant for large organizations.

Doc #023 Valued Touchpoint Workshop Charter Template
One-page charter template for capturing important and guiding information for a Workshop.

Doc #024 Valued Touchpoint Workshop Output Form
A sample form to capture Workshop output, and if applicable, present the output to a governance level for their response.

Doc #040 Macro Metrics
Summary of several common macro customer relationship metrics.

Doc #060 CEM Introduction Deck
An executive summary introduction to CEM foundations, concepts and benefits.

Doc #061 Hierarchy and definitions of key CEM terms
It is important to speak the same customer experience language. This is a hierarchy of key terms. Download a complete CEM eDictionary *http://www.touchpointguru.com/CEM-eDictionary.html*.

Visit www.TouchpointGuru.com/Members or www.TouchpointPower.com/Members.

These and other documents are available – Login Required.

Doc #500 Brigman's CX Correlation Formula
An original formula correlating results of "likelihood to recommend" question to top line revenue.

Doc #510 Customer Council Charter Template
Template sample.

Doc #520 20 Questions of a Valued Touchpoint Workshop
Following these 20 questions will produce the desired Workshop output.

Doc #560 CEM eDictionary
Complimentary eDictionary of terms used in TOUCHPOiNT POWER!

Index

243

245

Thank You!

Hank Brigman
Consultant, Coach, Speaker, Author

Building Customer-Centricity, Touchpoint by Touchpoint™

Customer Experience Management
Strategy • Implementation • Measurement

Phone: + 1 904.466.1805
Hank@TouchpointGuru.com
www.TouchpointGuru.com

Newsletter: *TOUCHPOiNTER*

Consultancy Web: *www.CxStrategiesInc.com*

Twitter: *@TouchpointGuru*

Speaker Member Profile: *National Speaker Association,*

Short Speaking Demo Video

Connect: *Linkedin Profile*

Facebook: *TouchpointGuru*